Reference Books

for Small and Medium-sized Libraries

2d edition, revised

Compiled by the
American Library Association
Reference Services Division
Ad Hoc Reference Books Review Committee

Charles R. Andrews, Chairman

Edited by
Richard A. Gray
and Judith Z. Cushman

AMERICAN LIBRARY ASSOCIATION
Chicago 1973

Library of Congress Cataloging in Publication Data

American Library Association. Reference Books
    Review Committee.
    Reference books for small and medium-sized
libraries.

    First ed. published in 1969 under title: Refer-
ence books for small and medium-sized public li-
braries, by the Basic Reference Books Committee,
American Library Association.
    1. Reference books—Bibliography. I. Gray,
Richard A., ed. II. Cushman, Judith Z., ed. III.
American Library Association. Basic Reference Books
Committee. Reference books for small and medium-
sized public libraries. IV. Title.
Z1035.1.A47   1973   011'.02   73-8906

    ISBN 0-8389-3140-5

Printed in the United States of America

Ad Hoc Reference Books Review Committee
Reference Services Division
American Library Association

ANN DRAIN
Librarian of Freiberger Library
Case Western Reserve University
Cleveland, Ohio

LYN HART
Assistant Coordinator, Adult Services
Enoch Pratt Free Library
Baltimore, Maryland

LORA LANDERS
Director of Reader Services
Hennepin County Library
Minneapolis, Minnesota

JOYCE F. SHIELDS
Coordinator, Reference and
   Interlibrary Loan Services
Suburban Library System
Oak Park Public Library
Oak Park, Illinois

CHARLES R. ANDREWS
Chairman
Assistant Director for Public Services
Case Western Reserve University
   Libraries
Cleveland, Ohio

Contents

CONTENTS

CONTENTS

CONTENTS

Preface

REFERENCE BOOKS FOR SMALL AND MEDIUM-SIZED LIBRARIES is an offspring of its parent publication prepared in the late 1960s by the Reference Services Division Basic Books Committee and published in 1969. Although proud of its heritage, as reflected in the resemblances of scope, format, and arrangement, this edition is a product of its own time. Like its predecessor it is designed as a helpful guide "for the purchase of reference collections for newly established libraries and for improving and expanding existing collections."

Potential Users

Although "public" has been dropped from the title, this publication is essentially public-library oriented, best suited to those libraries serving populations between 10,000 and 75,000. Those that serve communities of fewer than 10,000, with budgets permitting only the most basic reference sources, will doubtless do more selective buying and place greater reliance upon the resources of larger collections. On the other hand, those libraries serving communities exceeding 75,000 will probably rely on a larger range of choices than those suggested by this list.

Scope

The years intervening between editions not only have seen the publication of important new adult reference works but also have enabled users of the first edition to pinpoint some of the areas that needed revision or expansion. New titles and new editions have been added, especially those published between 1967 and 1971; some pre-1966 titles, missed in the first edition, have also been added.

Out-of-print titles, as well as dated items no longer providing current or reliable information, have been dropped; many still-useful titles have been carried over. The cut-off date for titles included is December 31, 1971, although some 1972 imprints have been included when they were available for examination. Reference books for children's collections are not within the scope of this list, nor as a general rule are textbooks, except in those cases where nothing else suitable exists in a particular field.

The Committee is aware that gaps in coverage may well exist, that faithful vade mecums have been missed. We hope that these are minimal and that other titles in the list can do the job as well, or perhaps better. As Alexander Pope said of perfection: "Whoever thinks a faultless piece to see / Thinks what ne'er was, nor is, nor e'er shall be." Nevertheless, we blame only ourselves for such oversights.

Format and Arrangement

The form of entry is standard: author, title, edition, publisher and date, paging (or volumes), price, and annotation. For serial publications the initial date and frequency of publication are generally given. Although prices were checked for accuracy, they are at best only approximate and have been included primarily as guidelines.

Numbering in the Contents refers to page numbers; numbering in the Index refers to entry numbers. The seventeen major subject categories follow approximately the same sequence as the broad divisions of the Dewey Decimal Classification, with some modification to place related subjects together. Items included under each major subject are grouped by subtopic, form, or both. An author-title index is provided.

Acknowledgments

The Chairman is deeply grateful to all the Committee members, whose wholehearted effort and saving sense of humor under trying circumstances made this book possible. The privilege of working with them underscored what professionalism at its finest implies.

Thanks are due also both Richard Gray, senior editor, ALA Publishing Services, whose skills are reflected in the annotations of all titles added since the first edition, and Pauline Cianciolo, executive editor of Publishing Services, for her genuine pleasantness in putting everything into perspective.

Finally, the thanks of everyone involved in this project must go to those publishers whose kind cooperation in providing many necessary review copies made a difficult job easier.

CHARLES R. ANDREWS
Chairman

1 Bibliographic and General Works

Bibliographical Sources

1 American book publishing record. Bowker, 1960– . Monthly. $16.75 a yr.
Cumulated from the "Weekly Record" section of *Publisher's Weekly,* the entries give full Library of Congress cataloging; additional information for revised, translated, and paperback editions; a brief descriptive annotation; the price; and publisher's address as needed. Contains author and title indexes. Cumulations with the same arrangement and scope are available for 1960–64 (4v.) at $89.95 and for 1965–69 (5v.) at $110. Annual volumes for 1965–69 may be bought individually at $28.50.

2 Books in print: an author-title-series index to the Publishers' trade list annual. Bowker, 1948– . Annually in Oct. 2v.: Authors; Titles. $27.50.
Lists all books in print in the United States. Author index volume gives date, price, and publisher. Title index volume gives only price and publisher; a directory of publishers and ISBN prefixes where available are included.

3 Subject guide to Books in print: a subject index to the Publishers' trade list annual. Bowker, 1957– . Annually in Oct. $23.50.
Arranges the books listed in Books in Print by Library of Congress subject headings with many cross references and subheadings. Each entry gives date, price, and publisher. Areas omitted are adult and juvenile fiction, poetry, drama, Bibles, and books priced at less than 25¢.

4 Cumulative book index: a world list of books in the English language. Wilson, 1898– . Monthly except Aug. Service basis.
Scope widened in 1928 to include books in English issued in the United States and Canada, and selected publications from other English-speaking places. Omits government documents and pamphlets. All entries (author, title, and subject) are arranged in a single alphabetical list. Full bibliographic data for author entries. For plan of cumulation consult the catalog of *Wilson Publications.*

5 Forthcoming books. Bowker, 1966– . Bimonthly. Paper $19.95 a yr.
A supplement to *Books in Print* which provides separate author and title indexes to books which are to appear in the next five-month period. Gives price, publisher, and expected publication date.

6   Subject guide to Forthcoming books. Bowker, 1967– . Bimonthly. Paper $8.95 a yr. Special combination rate for subscriptions to both *Forthcoming Books* and *Subject Guide,* $26.95 a yr.

Arranges in 200 subject areas those entries found in each *Forthcoming Books.*

7   Guide to microforms in print. Microcard Editions, 1961– . Annual. $6.

An alphabetically arranged guide to materials of United States publishers available on microfilm or other microforms. Does not list theses and dissertations. Essentially a price list.

8   Subject guide to microforms in print. Microcard Editions, 1962– . Biennial. $6.

Lists, under subject classifications, the material of *Guide to Microforms in Print.*

9   Paperbound books in print. Bowker, 1955– . Monthly with 3 (March, July, and Nov.) cumulative PBIP. $29.95 a yr.

The monthly magazine (now a separate publication to the cumulative edition) gives an annotated list, arranged under 26 basic subjects, of forthcoming paperbacks and includes a cumulating title index of those books published between the three cumulative issues. Also offers trade news and a feature article with accompanying bibliography. The cumulative volume is divided into three indexes: title, author, and subject.

10   Publishers' trade list annual. Bowker, 1873– . Annually in fall (1972 issue has 7v.) $29.50.

Compiles catalogs of more than 1900 publishers in alphabetical order.

Amount of information supplied by publisher varies. Volume 1 contains index of publishers and catalogs of small publishing houses.

Book Lists and Selection Aids

11   American reference books annual. Libraries Unlimited, 1970– . Annual. $19.75.

Describes in classified order reference books published in the United States or distributed here by U.S. distributors. Critical annotations and citations to reviews appearing elsewhere. More current than the Winchell *Supplements.* Index.

12   Booklist. American Library Assn., Sept. 1956– . Semimonthly Sept.–July; monthly in Aug. $12 a yr. (Formerly *The Booklist,* 1905–56, *Subscription Book Bulletin,* 1930–56, and *The Booklist and Subscription Books Bulletin,* 1956–69).

The Booklist is a book-selection tool, buying guide, and cataloging aid devoted to impartial, factual appraisals of new books recommended for library purchase. Descriptive, critical notes for each title summarize content and point out special uses or features. Complete ordering and cataloging information is given for each title. The Reference and Subscription Books Reviews give detailed, objective evaluations of reference books and sets—clearly recommended or not recommended—by ALA's Reference and Subscription Books Review Committee. Special sections and lists appear on fiction, series and editions, government publications, pamphlets, paperbacks, films, recordings, and on adult, young adult, and children's books. Also featured are bibliographies in fields of current interest. Subject-author-title index in each issue; semiannual and annual cumulative indexes.

13   Courtney, Winifred, F., ed. Reader's adviser. 11th ed. rev. and enl. Bowker, 1968–69. 2v. v.1, The best in literature, $20. v.2, Religion, science, philosophy, social sciences, history, and other subject areas, $18.50.

Designed primarily to help booksellers and librarians, this annotated guide lists, describes, and selects books in nearly every field of human knowledge, offering complete information on the various editions. Also useful for the student and general reader who will enjoy the background material and excerpted critical reviews as well as the bibliographic suggestions.

14   Choice: books for the liberal arts curriculum by subjects. v.1– . Assn. of College and Research Libraries, American Library Assn., 1964– . 11 issues a yr. $20 a yr.

Reviews approximately 6,000 titles a year. Reviewers are subject specialists who consistently compare the new title with similar and related books. Issues contain special bibliographic articles. Annual index.

15   Walsh, James Patrick. Home reference books in print: a comparative analysis, comp. by S. Padraig Walsh. Bowker, 1969. 284p. $10.95.

Describes and evaluates English-language dictionaries, world atlases, and subscription books. Provides such details as age suitability, subject coverage, and references to extended reviews. A good source for frequent inquiries concerning best volumes for home purchase.

16   Library journal. Bowker, 1876– . Semimonthly (Sept.–June); monthly (July–Aug.) $10 a yr.

A prime source for current book selection. The book review section in each issue contains about 200 signed reviews by librarians and others. Many special annual features. Also reviews of nonprint media. Indexes.

17   Publishers' weekly: the book industry journal. Bowker, 1872– . Weekly. $16.50 a yr. Each issue $1.

Provides news of the book trade. Of great value to librarians is the weekly listing of new books as they are being published. Full bibliographic information is given for each title. Spring, Summer, and Fall. Announcement issues ($7 a yr.) are also useful.

18   RQ. v.1– . Reference Services Division, American Library Assn. 1960– . Quarterly. Membership journal.

An excellent source for up-to-date signed reviews of current reference books by practicing reference librarians. Articles of interest to reference librarians.

19   Reference and subscription books reviews. American Library Assn. 1961– . Volumes (paper) for 1962–64, $2; 1964–66, $2.25; 1966–68, $2.25; 1968–70, $2.75; 1970–72, $3.50.

Compilation of reference book reviews which appeared in *The Booklist* and *Subscription Books Bulletin* for the years indicated. 1964–66 volume has a cumulative index for the years 1956–66. Title varies; before the 1968–70 volume, this series was known as the *Subscription Books Bulletin Reviews.*

20   Vertical file index. Wilson, 1935– . Monthly except Aug. $8 a yr.

Selected and current pamphlets of interest to the general library. Arrangement is by subject, with title, publisher, date, paging, and price. A descriptive note is usually given.

21   Walford, Albert J. Guide to reference material. 2d ed. The Library Assn. (distr. in U.S. by Bowker), 1966–70. 3v. $13.95 each.

The British counterpart and a useful supplement to Winchell's *Guide to Reference Books.* Classified arrangement with annotations and references to reviews. Scope is international but emphasis is on books published in Britain. The three volumes are: 1, *Science and Technology,* 1966; 2, *Philosophy, Psychology and Religion; Social and Historical Sciences,* 1968; and 3, *Generalia; Language and Literature; Arts,* 1970.

22   Wilson, H. W. *firm, publishers.* Public library catalog. Ed. by Estelle A. Fidell. 5th ed. Wilson, 1969. 1646p. $50; price includes 4 annual supplements, 1969–72. (Formerly *Standard Catalog for Public Libraries*).

11,000 titles in all fields selected with the small and medium-sized library in mind. Part 1 is a classified, annotated catalog with full bibliographic information. Part 2 is an author, title, subject, and analytical index to part 1. Part 3 is a directory of publishers and distributors. Paperbacks are now included when they are the only edition available.

23   Winchell, Constance M. Guide to reference books. 8th ed. American Library Assn., 1967. 741p. $15. Ed. by Eugene P. Sheehy: 1st supplement, 1965–66 (1968), 122p. $3.50; 2d supplement, 1967–68 (1970), 165p. $4; 3d supplement, 1969–70 (1972), 190p. $4.50.

This edition of an important reference tool and selection aid lists about 7500 reference books basic to research and serves as a manual for the library assistant and research worker. Beginning with the second, the supplement series has had a cumulative index.

Book Reviews

24   Book review digest. Wilson, 1906– . Monthly except Feb. and July, with annual cumulation. Service basis.

An index to current reviews in approximately 75 English and American periodicals, with excerpts and digests. Each issue has a title and subject index. Issues for 1905–59 are available at prices ranging from $5 to $15 per volume. Annuals 1960–68 and 1969 sold on service basis.

25   Book review index. Gale, 1965– . Annual. $30.

Differs from *Book Review Digest* in that it is solely an author index with only review sources cited. Indexes all reviews in approximately 200 sources. Publication ceased as of 1968, but may be resumed in 1973. The 1969, 1970, and 1971 volumes may be published in 1973, 1974, and 1975, in addition to the monthly schedule with annual cumulations.

Directories

26   American book trade directory.

Ed. by Eleanor F. Steiner-Prag. Bowker, 1915– . Biennial. $27.50. Includes lists of publishers in the United States, former publishing companies, dealers in foreign books, exporters importers, wholesalers, and an international directory of booksellers. The former index to wholesalers has been absorbed by a new index to retail booksellers. Bookstores are arranged under state and city with specialty of each noted.

27 American library directory: a classified list of libraries, with personnel and statistical data. Ed. by Eleanor F. Steiner-Prag and Helaine MacKeigan. Bowker, 1923– . Biennial. $30.

Includes United States and Canadian public, college, and special libraries arranged by state, city, and institution. Subject strengths are indicated.

28 Bowker annual of library and book trade information. Sponsored by the Council of National Library Assns. Bowker, 1956– . Annual.

An extremely useful compendium of statistical and directory information relating to most aspects of librarianship and the book trade. Index.

29 Kruzas, Anthony T. Directory of special libraries and information centers. Gale, 1968. 3v. $84.50. v.1, Directory of special libraries and informational centers. 1408p. $28.50. v.2, Geographic-personnel index. 503p. $23.50. v.3, New special libraries (a periodic supplement). $32.50.

Volume 1 is a classified directory of special libraries that are independent agencies and those that are subunits of larger institutions. Provides particulars

on staff, foundation date, subject strengths, publications, etc.; subject index. Volume 2 is arranged by state and city; separate personnel index. Volume 3 consists of a binder and four supplements.

30 Literary market place, the business directory of American book publishing. Bowker, 1940– . Annual. Paper $14.95.

Useful for a variety of publishing data. Includes information on publishers, book manufacturers, book reviewers, literary agents, literary awards and fellowships, and periodical agencies. Helpful to the amateur and professional writer in selecting a publisher. For the same categories of information on an international basis, consult *International Literary Market Place* (Bowker, 1965– . Annual. Paper $10).

Periodical and Newspaper Directories and Indexes

31 Ayer, *firm, newspaper advertising agents.* Ayer directory of newspapers, magazines and trade publications. Ayerpress, 1880– . Annual. $40.

Geographical list of periodical publications in the United States and its territories, Canada, Bermuda, the Republic of Panama, and the Republic of the Philippines. Size, format, periodicity, and political sympathies are indicated as well as economic, statistical, and climatic information for each state and city. Classified lists include agricultural, collegiate, foreign language, Negro, religious, fraternal, trade and technical, labor, etc., publications. Maps. Indexed.

32 Directory of little magazines,

small presses, and underground newspapers. Dust Books, 1966– . Annual. $2.50.

A useful directory for titles not listed in *Ayer's* or *Ulrich's*. Provides addresses, editors, scope, and fields of interests of periodicals and newspapers and indicates payment schedules for accepted contributions.

33   Editor and Publisher, *periodical.* International yearbook: the encyclopedia of the newspaper industry. Editor and Publisher, 1960– . Annual (in March). Paper $12.

A geographical listing of newspapers, giving circulation and advertising information. Includes information on many foreign newspapers, national, and press associations, Better Business Bureaus, awards, and many aspects of the newspaper industry.

34   Irregular serials and annuals: an international directory. Ed. by Emery I. Kattay. 2d ed. Bowker, 1972. 1350p. $38.50.

A classified directory of those serials issued irregularly, annually, or less frequently than once a year. Arranged under 230 subject headings. Index. Special feature: International Standard Serial Numbers (ISSN) for all serials listed in *Irregular Serials and Annuals* and in *Ulrich's International Periodicals Directory.*

35   Katz, William Armstrong, and Gargal, Barry. Magazines for libraries, for the general reader and public school, junior college and college libraries. 2d ed. Bowker, 1972, 822p. $25.

A classified and critically annotated list of magazines designed to display for each title: purpose, audience, scope, and reading level. Full order information is given as is a statement of where each title is indexed. Title index.

36   New York Times index. New York Times Co., 1913– . Twice a month, $87.50; annual cumulation, $87.50; combined service, $150.

Summarizes and classifies news alphabetically by subjects, persons, and organizations. Helpful in locating articles not only in the *New York Times* but also in other papers, as entries establish the date of events. Indexes for earlier volumes may be obtained from the publisher: 1851–1906, 9v. $44.50 each; v. for 1907–12 in prep.

37   Readers' guide to periodical literature. Wilson, 1900– . Semimonthly Sept.–June; monthly July and Aug., with quarterly and permanent bound annual cumulations. $35 a yr.

An author-subject index to about 160 general and nontechnical magazines. Essential in any library. Volumes 1–29 (1900–70) are in print at $32 a volume.

38   Muller, Robert H.; Spahn, Theodore Jurgen; and Spahn, Janet M. From radical left to extreme right: a bibliography of current periodicals of protest, controversy, advocacy or dissent, with dispassionate content summaries to guide librarians and other educators through the polemic fringe. 2d ed. rev. & enl. v.1. Campus Publishers, 1970. 510p. $14.75; paper $13.75. Spahn, Theodore Jurgen; Spahn, Janet; and Muller, Robert H. v.2. Scarecrow, 1972. p.511–1000

(continues the pagination of v.1). $12.50.

A classified, fully annotated bibliography of 674 periodicals about which satisfactory information is often impossible to find elsewhere. In addition to full bibliographic data, address, price, and format for each periodical, there are contents summaries of editorial positions. A unique feature of this work is that the compilers afforded each periodical's editor an opportunity to comment on the contents summary that had been prepared for the journal. That comment, when it was forthcoming, appears under the heading "feedback." The classification is by category of polemical concern and advocacy, e.g. Marxist socialist left, women's liberation, peace, race supremacy, etc. Indexes.

39 Ulrich's International periodicals directory. 14th ed. Bowker, 1971. 2v. 2016p. (continuously paged) $42.50.

A classified list of current domestic and foreign periodicals. Provides complete publishing and subscription information. Indications of where, if anywhere, each is indexed or abstracted. Separate listing of new periodicals, 1969–71. Key to subject headings. Title and subject index.

40 The underground press directory. William D. Lutz, 1968– . Annual. $3.

An alphabetical listing of underground or alternative or counter-culture periodicals and newspapers. Information consists of full mailing address. A necessary supplement to *Ayer's* and *Ulrich's*.

41 Union list of serials in the United States and Canada. 3d ed. Wilson, 1965. 5v. $120.

A guide to the location of periodical files and the availability of copies either through interlibrary loan or photocopy in 956 American and Canadian libraries. This edition covers 156,499 serial titles in existence through Dec. 1949.

42 U.S. Library of Congress. New serial titles, 1950–60: a supplement to the Union list of serials. 3d ed. Library of Congress, 1961, 1966. 2v. $56.25 the set. Continued by 8 monthly issues, 4 quarterly issues, and annual cumulative. $115 a yr.

Lists and locates newly available serials, and gives information on name changes, mergers, and cessation of periodicals. A three-volume compilation for 1961–65 is available from Bowker at $47.50. For the period 1966–69, the complete set of *New Serial Titles* will consist of the 1950–60 and the 1961–65 cumulative volumes as supplemented by the latest annual cumulation and the monthly and quarterly issues.

Government Publications

43 Bernier, Bernard A., and David, Charlotte M., comps. Popular names of U.S. government reports: a catalog. Rev. and enl. ed. Govt. Print. Off., 1970. 43p. 55¢

44 U.S. Superintendent of Documents. Price list of government publications. Govt. Print. Off., 1898– . Single copies free; sets of 20 for $1.

A useful guide to inexpensive and current materials, covering about 50 different topics, published by the federal government.

45 U.S. Library of Congress. Processing Dept. Monthly checklist of state publications. Govt. Print. Off., 1910– . $8 a yr. Annual index; price varies.

Lists official publications of the various states with price and relevant bibliographic data. (State libraries and state library associations frequently publish bibliographies for their own states.)

46 U.S. Superintendent of Documents. Monthly catalog of United States government publications. Govt. Print. Off., 1895– . $7 a yr. with index.

More extensive guide than the *Price List* (no. 44). Each issue has a subject index which is cumulated in December.

2 Encyclopedias

▶ Each library reference collection will need one or more encyclopedias, depending upon its public and upon the purchases and location of the Children's Room, if there is a separate room for this age group. It is advisable in a larger reference collection to buy consistently the annuals for the encyclopedias purchased. In some smaller collections, this may not be necessary. If several encyclopedias are purchased, buy sets at staggered intervals, so that there will always be a recent one.

In the following list, annotations are descriptive. There is no attempt to indicate priority among the multivolume sets, but the following title may be used as a guide to the evaluation of encyclopedias.

47 Walsh, S. Padraig, comp. General encyclopedias in print: a comparative analysis. Bowker, 1968– . Annual. Paper $3.

As a practical guide for evaluating encyclopedias, this small handbook describes in detail the arrangement, age, suitability, history, subject coverage, reviews, etc., of the main general knowledge encyclopedias published. A consensus of opinion chart, by professional librarians and educators, lists those encyclopedias recommended and those not recommended.

48 Collier's Encyclopedia. Crowell-Collier Educ. Corp. (distr. by Collier–Macmillan School and Library Service). 24v. $242.50.

An adult encyclopedia suitable for junior and senior high school students as well as for college and university students. Articles are well developed, well presented, and well illustrated. Arrangement is alphabetical, letter by letter. The scholarly, signed articles vary in length according to importance of subject treated. The set is especially useful for its coverage of politics, biography, fine arts, religion, philosophy, the classics, science, and technology. Small topical maps and large (many multicolored) maps with adjacent gazetteer information accompany articles on states, provinces, and countries. The list of contributors appears in volume 1 and notes the qualifications and writings of each specialist. Volume 24 contains the bibliography, a comprehensive, analytical index, and a study guide designed to aid the reader seeking to enlarge his knowledge on a particular subject. Bibliographies are listed under broad subject fields, explicitly subdivided, with title entries arranged under broad or narrow subjects according to the scope of the books listed; generally the books begin at high school level and progress through college and postcollege levels, with easier or general works treated first. Continuous revision program, with several printings a year, assures up-to-dateness. The second 1971 set contains 1970 census figures. This set costs $307.

49   Collier's Yearbook. $10.75. Supplement and annual survey.

50   Compton's Encyclopedia and fact-index. Encyclopaedia Britannica (distr. by Encyclopaedia Britannica Educ. Corp.). 24v. $144, plus delivery charge.

A juvenile encyclopedia for home and school use. Designed to meet requirements of school curricula and interests of children from grade 4 through high school. Can be used by parents and teachers who wish to help children help themselves, and contains articles on important phases of family life written for adults. Arrangement is letter by letter, and each volume, consisting of one or more complete letters of the alphabet, is divided into two parts. (As of the 1968 set, some letters take two volumes.) The main text (part 1) is an alphabetical arrangement of principal articles on broad subjects. These are well illustrated with pictures, charts, and diagrams, and contain cross references. Articles on states include a fact summary and maps with gazetteer information. A new section, the "State Profile," shows state symbols and local sites, lists famous natives, and gives a candid view of the state in a short essay. Fact summaries now also follow articles on countries, continents, and Canadian provinces. Coverage on scientific subjects is good. Some of the main text articles contain reference-outlines which refer to other articles in the set, and bibliographies which refer to significant books in print; the bibliographies for major articles are divided into

two lists, one for younger readers and the other for advanced students and teachers. Part 2 is a Fact-Index which incorporates dictionary type of information and brief biographical sketches with an analytical index of all text and illustrative material in that particular volume. Articles are not signed, but the speciality of each contributor is noted in the list of consultants and contributors in volume 1. Maintains a continuous revision program with several printings a year. Formerly called *Compton's Pictured Encyclopedia and Fact-Index.*

51   Compton's Yearbook. $7.95. Supplement and annual record.

52   Encyclopedia Americana. Grolier. 30v. $375.

A popular adult encyclopedia suitable for junior and senior high school as well as college and university students. Arrangement is alphabetical, word by word. Articles are well developed and presented in a style easy to understand. For the most part the articles are short, but those on subjects of major importance are lengthy and signed by the specialist who wrote them. Articles are well illustrated. Bibliographies appear at the end of major articles and list authoritative sources for further information; for longer articles, bibliographies are subdivided into topics relating to sections of the article. Large multicolored maps with gazetteer information and smaller topical maps accompany text on states and countries. The last volume contains an illustrated section of chronological world events for the preceding five years and a comprehensive, analytical index which may be used as a study guide. Continuous revision with several printings a year.

Valuable for its articles on science, technology, biography, topics of American interests, and digests of opera, drama, and books. The list of contributors in volume 1 indicates the specific articles each contributor has written for the set.

53 Americana annual. $7.95. Supplement and annual survey.

54 Encyclopaedia Britannica. Encyclopaedia Britannica (distr. by Encyclopaedia Britannica Educ. Corp.). 24v. $299.50, plus delivery charge.

The most famous, scholarly, and oldest English-language adult encyclopedia still in existence; suitable for high school, college, and university students, and mature adults. Arrangement is alphabetical, letter by letter, in broad subject articles with many subheads and in shorter articles on specific topics. Lengthy articles, prefaced with a table of contents, have cross references and include excellent bibliographies of works in English and some in foreign languages. The articles are signed with the initials of the contributing specialist, who is identified and whose qualifications are noted in volume 1. The last volume is a comprehensive and definitive Index, making any specific information in the set easily and exactly located. The Index volume also contains a world atlas of over 200 multicolored maps and an atlas index. Well illustrated. Maintains systematic and continuous revision, and updating of important subjects for each annual printing. Especially noted for coverage on civics, literature, science, art, geography, biography, and history.

55 Britannica book of the year. $8.95, plus delivery charge. Supplement and annual survey.

56 World book encyclopedia. Field Enterprises. 20v. $184.30; $144 to libraries.

A good encyclopedia for young people from elementary grades through high school, and popular also as a general adult encyclopedia. Articles are written at the school level for which specific subjects are likely to be studied. Arrangement is alphabetical, word by word. Articles are clear, concise, and factual, the length depending on the importance of the subject treated, and they are signed. The list of contributors in volume 1 gives the title of articles each specialist has contributed to the set. Well-illustrated, multicolored maps have their own index on adjacent pages. While there is no index to the set, there are copious cross references. Major articles contain study aids: lists of related articles, frequently an outline, pertinent questions for understanding comprehension, and separate lists of books for further reading for young readers, and for older readers. Also features different visual aids. Especially useful for scientific subjects, literature, art, and biography. Maintains a continuous revision program.

57 World book year book, an annual supplement. $6.95.

3 Philosophy and Religion

Dictionaries, Encyclopedias, and Handbooks

58 Brandon, S. G. F., gen. ed. A dictionary of comparative religion. Scribner's, 1970. 704p. $17.50.
A compendium of concisely written, authoritative articles. Contains bibliographies and a detailed subject index.

59 Catholic dictionary (The Catholic encyclopaedic dictionary). Ed. by Donald Attwater. 3d ed. Macmillan, 1961. 552p. Paper $2.45.
Contains brief but complete definitions of religious terms and associations, including histories of the latter when necessary. Ecclesiastical calendar of the Church, and titles and modes of address are also given.

60 Encyclopedia Judaica. Macmillan, 1972. 16v. $500.
A completely new encyclopedic survey of Judaic culture, utilizing the results of modern scholarship in archeology, history, and Biblical exegesis. Indispensable but does not supersede the *Jewish Encyclopedia* which should be retained for its older perspectives.

61 Encyclopedia of philosophy. Paul Edwards, ed. in chief. Macmillan, 1967. 8v. $219.50.
Scholarly work within the understanding of the general reader. For all periods covers both Oriental and Western philosophers, concepts, and schools of philosophy. Useful also for investigating peripheral fields in the sciences and social sciences. Signed articles; contributors represent subject authority on international level. Good bibliographies follow articles. Full cross referencing is sometimes lacking, but there is a good index. Major contribution to a field where a new encyclopedic work has long been needed.

62 Hastings, James, with the assistance of Selbie, John A., and Gray, Louis H. Encyclopaedia of religion and ethics. Scribner's, 1908–27. 13v. (12 text, 1 index) $220 (by subscription only)
Despite its age, still the standard comprehensive work in English. Includes discussions of religions and ethical systems as these relate to anthropology, folklore, psychology, etc. Full bibliographies.

63 Magill, Frank N., ed. Masterpieces of world philosophy in summary form. Harper, 1961. 1166p. $11.95; lib. bdg. $9.89.
Synopses of basic philosophical works from ancient to modern times. Includes a glossary of philosophical terms.

64 Mead, Frank S. Handbook of denominations in the United States. 5th ed. Abingdon, 1970. 265p. $3.95.

Handbook arranged by denomination, giving the history and basic beliefs of each. Glossary, bibliography, index, and a list of the denominations' headquarters.

65 New Catholic encyclopedia. Prepared by an editorial staff at the Catholic University of America. McGraw-Hill, 1967. 15v. $550; $450 to libraries.

Highly objective, modern, and ecumenical in tone. Retains a high level of scholarship, yet is generally more readable than the old. Many contributors are non-Catholic. Partially, though not completely, replaces and supersedes the *Catholic Encyclopedia* (Gilmary Society, 1907–22, 1950–54. 18v. O.P.) which should be retained for older, historically important points of view and formulations.

66 Oxford dictionary of the Christian church. Ed. by F. L. Cross. Oxford Univ. Pr., 1957. 1492p. $17.50.

Scholarly and useful dictionary for terms and names associated with the Christian faith. Old Testament names are also included. Bibliographies at end of most articles.

67 Schaff-Herzog encyclopedia. Twentieth century encyclopedia of religious knowledge: an extension of the New Schaff-Herzog encyclopedia of religious knowledge. Ed. in chief, Lefferts A. Loetscher. Baker Book House, 1955. 2v. $19.95.

Description of religious affairs and personalities of the first half of the twentieth century. Concise signed articles, many with bibliography. Although a supplement to the *New Schaff-*

Herzog Encyclopedia, this can be used independently.

68 Wedeck, H. E., and Baskin, Wade. Dictionary of pagan religions. Philosophical Library, 1971. 363p. $10.

A dictionary of pre-Christian credal systems and practices which have persisted in Europe and the Middle East despite the dominance of the Christian church.

69 Weiser, Francis X. Handbook of Christian feasts and customs: the year of the Lord in liturgy and folklore. Harcourt, 1958. 366p. $5.95.

Explains Christian feasts with special emphasis on liturgy. Index. Bibliographies.

Yearbooks

70 American Jewish year book. Jewish Pub., 1899– . $10.

International in scope. Embraces all aspects of Jewish activities, and includes population statistics, directories of organizations, and Jewish periodicals, necrology, American Jewish bibliography, and Jewish calendar.

71 Catholic almanac. Doubleday, 1904– . $4.95.

Basic current information about the Catholic church and its members. Includes such dividends as a list of Catholic periodicals, books, writers' market, theater, radio and TV programs, and awards. Formerly entitled *National Catholic Almanac.*

72 Official Catholic directory. Kenedy, 1886– . Annually in May. $35.

For each diocese, lists churches,

schools, hospitals, clergy, and religious orders. Also gives statistical information, places in the United States having resident pastor, alphabetical list of clergy, Eastern rites, and necrology.

73   Yearbook of American churches: information on all faiths in the U.S.A. Ed. by Constant H. Jacquet, Jr. National Council of Churches, 1916– . $8.95.

Directory and statistical information on many religious organizations and service agencies; accredited seminaries, colleges, and universities and religious periodicals.

Bibles

Dictionaries and Encyclopedias

74   Gehman, Henry Snyder, ed. The new Westminster dictionary of the Bible. Westminster, 1970. 1027p. $10.95.

Long a standard authority since first publication in 1898, this new edition incorporates the archaeological discoveries as well as the textual criticism of the last twenty-five years.

75   Hastings, James, ed. Dictionary of the Bible. Rev. ed. by Frederick C. Grant and H. H. Rowley. Scribner's, 1963. $15.

Identification of people and places found in the Bible, as well as explanation of biblical terms. Based on Revised Standard Version.

76   McKenzie, John L. Dictionary of the Bible. Bruce, 1965. 954p. $17.95; paper $5.95.

Highly authoritative treatment by a Catholic scholar. Balanced, objective, ecumenical, and based on solid archaeological research. Contains an up-to-

date, although brief, bibliography. Good illustrations and maps. Complements Hastings, but is more appropriate for the general reader.

Concordances and Quotation Books

►   There are several concordances corresponding to each of the various versions of the Bible. In the following selection, the title or the note indicates that version of the Bible on which each concordance is based.

77   Cruden, Alexander. Cruden's Unabridged concordance to the Old and New Testaments and the Apocrypha. Baker Book House, 1953. 719p. $6.95.

King James version. The special value of this work is that Cruden provides an index to the Apocrypha. Note that some reprints of the work omit the Apocrypha concordance.

78   Ellison, John W., ed. Nelson's Complete concordance of the Revised Standard version Bible. Nelson, 1957. 2157p. $20.

The most complete concordance of this version. Computer-produced.

79   Joy, Charles R., ed. Harper's Topical concordance. Rev. and enl. ed. Harper, 1962. 628p. $8.95.

King James version. A subject, rather than a word, concordance. For example, one can check under such contemporary concepts as "integration" to find pertinent Bible passages.

80   Stevenson, Burton E. Home book of Bible quotations. Harper, 1949. 645p. $12.50.

Quotations from the King James version of the Bible, including Apocrypha, are arranged by subject. Includes a word concordance with citation to book, chapter, and verse in the Bible.

81 Strong, James. Exhaustive concordance of the Bible. Abingdon, 1958. 1340, 262, 126, 79p. (4v. in 1). $15,75; thumb-indexed $17.

Main part of the book contains the most complete concordance to the Bible. Other parts are the comparative concordance of the authorized and revised versions of the text of the canonical books of the Holy Scriptures, the concise dictionary of the words in the Hebrew Bible with their renderings in the Authorized English version, and a Greek dictionary of the New Testament.

82 Thompson, Newton W., and Stock, Raymond. Complete concordance to the Bible (Douay version). 4th rev. and enl. ed. Herder, 1945. 1914p. $21.

Needed for location of texts in the Douay Bible.

83 The Zondervan expanded concordance. Zondervan Publishing House, 1968. 1848p. $14.95.

A key word index to seven major versions of the Bible: King James, Amplified Bible, Berkeley version, J. B. Phillips' New Testament in Modern English, Revised Standard, New English Bible, and English Revised. A necessary addition in view of the recent proliferation of new versions.

Atlases

84 May, Herbert G., and others, ed. Oxford Bible atlas. Oxford Univ. Pr., 1962. 144p. $4.95; paper $2.50.

Includes physical, historical, and archeological maps. Text gives history with dates of rulers. Gazetteer lists names on maps with Bible references wherever applicable.

85 Wright, George Ernest, and Filson, Floyd Vivian. Westminster historical atlas to the Bible. Rev. ed. Westminster, 1956. 130p. $7.50.

Contains maps, text, illustrations, and chronological outlines of ancient history. Besides a good general index there is an index to modern place-names and a tabulation of biblical sites. Places named in the Bible can be readily located. Also includes index of Arabic names identified with biblical places in Syria and Palestine. Revision takes into account the discovery of the Dead Sea Scrolls.

Other Sacred Writings

86 Koran. Trans. by J. M. Rodwell. Dutton [n.d.]. (Everyman's ed.) 506p. $2.95; lib. ed. $3.80.

87 Warren, Henry Clarke, ed. and trans. Buddhism in translations: passages selected from the Buddhist sacred books and translated from the original Pāli into English. Atheneum, 1963. 496p. Paper $2.95.

Mythology and Folklore

Indexes

88 Eastman, Mary Huse. Index to fairy tales, myths and legends. 2d ed. rev. and enl. Faxon, 1926. 610p. $9. Supplement, 1937. 563p. $9; 2d supplement, 1952. 370p. $9.

Although this is an essential reference book for the children's department, it is a valuable source for the location of much folklore and fairy-tale material and should be available in adult book collections as well.

Dictionaries, Encyclopedias, and Handbooks

89   Botkin, Benjamin Albert, ed. Treasury of American folklore. Foreword by Carl Sandburg. Crown, 1944. 932p. $5.95.

Humorous anecdotes and jests, tall tales and yarns, ballads and songs, legends of the backwoods, badmen, heroes and demigods, boosters and knockers are included in this collection. Index of authors, titles, and first lines of songs; index of subjects and names.

90   Brown, Raymond L. A book of superstitions. Taplinger, 1970. 116p. $3.95.

Ancient and modern superstitions arranged under broad rubrics such as amulets, gambling, numbers, and symbols. Sources are not cited. No index.

91   Bulfinch, Thomas. Bulfinch's Mythology: The age of fable; The age of chivalry; Legends of Charlemagne. 2d. rev. ed. Crowell, 1970. 1056p. $6.95.

Legends and myths from Greek, Roman, and Eastern mythologies and stories of King Arthur and Charlemagne. This edition features an appendix describing the archeological finds at the sites referred to in the classical texts. Dictionary-index.

92   Ostwalt, Sabine G. Concise encyclopedia of Greek and Roman mythology. Follett, 1969. 313p. $3.95; paper $2.95.

A superior system of cross references renders immediately accessible in clear alphabetical order an extraordinary amount of data on classical myths within the compass of a small, inexpensive volume.

93   Tripp, Edward. Crowell's Handbook of classical mythology. Crowell, 1970. 631p. $10.

Includes discussions and analyses of the major writers of antiquity, references to whose works are cited in the widely owned *Loeb Classical Library*. Index.

94   Frazer, *Sir* James G. New Golden bough; a new abridgement of the classic work. Ed. by Theodor H. Gaster. S. G. Phillips, 1959. 738p. $12.95; paper $1.95 (New Amer. Lib.).

Excellent interpretation of the evolution of beliefs and customs related to magic and religion. Satisfactory substitute for Frazer's original multivolume work, still available from St. Martin's Press at $125 the set.

95   Funk and Wagnalls Standard dictionary of folklore, mythology and legend. Maria Leach, ed.; Jerome Fried, assoc. ed. Funk, 1949–50. 2v. Boxed $25.

Embraces various aspects of folklore. With many anthropologists and sociologists among the contributors, the ethnic rather than the literary side is emphasized.

96   Gayley, Charles M. Classic myths in English literature and in art. Rev. ed. Ginn, 1939. 597p. $7.95.

Although not revised since 1939, Gayley is still an excellent source for the explanation of Greek, Roman, Norse, and German myths.

97   Norton, Daniel S., and Rushton, Peters. Classical myths in English

literature. Greenwood, 1952. 444p. $14.50.

Characters and events from Greek and Roman myths, alphabetically arranged, with illustrations of their use in classical and in English and American literatures. Literary references are indexed.

98   Radford, Edwin. Encyclopedia of superstitions, rev. by Christina Hale. Rev. and enl. ed. Dufour, 1969. 384p. $8.95.

An encyclopedia dictionary of superstitions presently found or recently defunct in the British Isles. A detailed motif index brings together related and analogous superstitious beliefs.

99   Robbins, Rossell Hope. Encyclopedia of witchcraft and demonology. Crown, 1959. 576p. $10.

Facts, history, and legend from 1450 to 1750. Extensive bibliography. Illustrations.

100 Sykes, Egerton, comp. Everyman's dictionary of non-classical mythology. 3d new rev. ed. Dutton, 1965. 280p. $5.

Characters, legends, deities, and place-names from mythology outside the classical world are listed in one alphabet. Geographical coverage includes Europe, Asia, Middle East, Africa, the Pacific, and North and South America.

4 Psychology

Bibliographies

101 Harvard University. Harvard list of books in psychology, comp. and annotated by psychologists in Harvard University. 4th ed. Harvard Univ. Pr., 1971. 108p. Paper $2.75.

A standard classified list of books chosen as "important and valuable in psychology at the present time." Index.

Dictionaries, Encyclopedias, and Handbooks

102 Baldwin, James M., ed. Dictionary of philosophy and psychology. Peter Smith, 1960. 3v. v.1, $15; v.2, $15; v.3 in 2 pts., $12.50 each.

Reprint of 1925 edition; old but still valid. Volumes 1 and 2 comprise the *Dictionary of Philosophical and Psychological Terms* and include brief biographical information about philosophers, theologists, and persons whose lives may be of interest to psychologists. Volume 3 is Benjamin Rand's *Bibliography of Philosophy, Psychology and Cognate Subjects*. Illustrations, plates, and diagrams.

103 Ellis, Albert, and Ararbanel, Albert, eds. The encyclopedia of sexual behavior. Hawthorn, 1967. 1072p. O.P. Ace Books, 1969. 5v. Paper 95¢ each.

The paperback reprint has the title: *Aspects of Sexuality.*

A collection of signed authoritative articles, approximately 100 in number, comprehensively covering major topics, e.g. adolescent sexuality, sex differences, transvestism. Arranged by major topic. Analytical guide to contents and a detailed subject index.

104 English, Horace B., and English, Ava C. Comprehensive dictionary of psychological and psychoanalytical terms: a guide to usage. McKay, 1958. 594p. $10.75.

Most up-to-date one-volume dictionary of psychological and psychoanalytical terms. Pronunciations are given.

105 Eysenck, Hans Jurgen, ed. Encyclopedia of psychology. Herder & Herder, 1972. 3v. $75.

A scientific, authoritative encyclopedic survey of psychology. Contains approximately 5,000 entries ranging from extensive articles to succinct definitions. Bibliographies appended to the major articles.

106 Goldenson, Robert M. Encyclopedia of human behavior: psychology, psychiatry, and mental health. Doubleday, 1970. 2v. $24.95.

For both the informed layman and the professional, this work provides valuable initial discussions and analyses. Bibliographies.

107 Hopke, William E., ed. Dictionary of personnel and guidance terms, including professional agencies and associations. Ferguson, 1968. 464p. $10.95.
A dictionary of terms used in the modern practice of personnel and guidance work. Definitions are keyed to readings in the bibliography. A classified listing of terms by categories.

108 Mental measurements yearbook. Ed. by Oscar K. Buros. 6th ed. Gryphon, 1965. 1714p. $32.50.
The sixth "yearbook" covers the period of 1959 to 1964 and supplements but does not supersede the previous five editions. Consists of two sections: psychological tests and their reviews; and books on all phases of testing and their reviews. Index.

109 Rycroft, Charles. A critical dictionary of psychoanalysis. Basic Books, 1969. 189p. $5.95.
Concise definitions of technical psychoanalytic terms, everyday terms given specialized meanings in analysis and terms given varying meanings by different psychoanalytic schools. Bibliography.

110 Woodworth, Robert S., and Sheehan, Mary R. Contemporary schools of psychology. 3d ed. Ronald, 1964. 457p. $7.
Standard textbook in the field, providing excellent material about each school of psychology. Indexed. Illustrated.

5 Business and Economics

Bibliographies and Indexes

111 Business periodicals index. Wilson, 1958– . Monthly except July, with annual cumulation. Service basis.
A subject index to periodicals in the fields of accounting, advertising, automation, banking, communications, economics, finance and investments, insurance, labor, management, marketing, taxes, etc. When the *Industrial Arts Index* was divided into two separate indexes in 1958, *Business Periodicals Index* and *Applied Science and Technology Index* were established.

112 Coman, Edwin T. Sources of business information. 2d ed. Univ. of California Pr., 1964. 330p. $8.50.
This guide to the literature of business is a standard in its field. Arranged under subject divisions. Many of the titles are annotated. Indexed.

113 Johnson, H. Webster, and McFarland, Stuart S. How to use the business library, 3d ed. South-Western, 1964. 160p. Paper $2.
A basic, inexpensive guide to the use of any business library, as well as a fine extensive listing of the important books in the field. Sections on government publication and trade and commercial organizations are very good. Well annotated and indexed.

Directories

► Every reference collection should include the following basic tools, if they exist, for the library's own city, county, and state: alphabetical and classified telephone directories for local and adjacent areas; industrial directory for the city, county, or state; directory of directors of corporations for the local area; directory of labor unions for the local area.

114 American register of exporters and importers. American Register of Exporters and Importers Corp., 1946– . Annual. $20.
List of U.S. firms from which specific products may be purchased by foreign countries, arranged by product with alphabetical listing of exporters, importers, and export agents.

115 Directory of franchising organizations. 12th ed. Pilot Industries, 1971. 180p. $2.
Arranged alphabetically by product categories. Lists about 400 American firms which offer franchise opportunities and for each briefly notes needed investment, territories open, etc.

116 Dun and Bradstreet, *firm, publishers.* Middle market directory. Dun and Bradstreet, 1964– . Annual. $75.

Lists industrial and other business concerns having a net worth of $500,000 to $999,999. Alphabetical by company name, giving addresses and officers. SIC (Standard Industrial Classification) numbers and number of employees. Geographical and SIC indexes.

117 ——— Million dollar directory. Dun and Bradstreet, 1959– . Annual. $108.

Lists industrial and other business concerns having a net worth of $1 million or more. Alphabetical by company name, giving addresses and officers. SIC (Standard Industrial Classification) numbers and number of employees. Geographical and SIC indexes.

118 Fortune, *periodical*. Fortune directory of 500 largest U.S. industrial corporations. Time, Inc., 1930– . Annual (in May). $1.

Also available as a reprint with *Fortune Directory of 501 to 1000 U.S. Industrial Corporations* (from the June issue) for $3.75. The first also lists largest banks, retailers, transportation, life insurance, and utilities companies.

119 Klein, Bernard, ed. Guide to American directories: a guide to the major business directories of the United States, covering all industrial professional and mercantile categories. 8th ed. Klein, 1971. 465p. $30.

A directory of directories. Arrangement is by subject, covering more than 300 categories. Under each entry there is descriptive information, price, and frequency of publication. Indexed also by name.

120 International yellow pages. Donnelley, 1963– . Annual. $20.

Lists businesses, professional firms, and manufacturers in 150 countries. Arrangement is first by country and then by product or service headings which are designated by numbers. Index of headings. Information given for each company consists of full name, mailing address, and telephone number. A multi-lingual publication, the work includes separate subject heading indexes in French, Spanish, and German.

121 Poor's Register of corporations, directors and executives. Standard and Poor's Corp., 1928– . Annual. $105.

Lists by firm name executive rosters and business telephone numbers of 33,000 companies in the United States and Canada. The second section gives brief biographical information on approximately 75,000 directors and executives, arranged in alphabetical "Who's Who" order.

122 Thomas register of American manufacturers. Thomas Publ., 1905– . Annual. 11v. $44.75. v.1–6, Product classifications; v.7, Alphabetical list of manufacturers; v.8, Product index, advertisers index, brand names and trademarks, boards of trade, and commercial organizations; v.9–11, Catalogs of manufacturers.

National purchase guide, supplying names and addresses of manufacturers, producers, importers, and other sources of supply in all lines and in all sections of the United States. Symbols show minimum capital of each firm. Volumes 9–11 contain manufacturers' catalogs in alphabetical order and are referred to as "THOMCAT"—Thomas Register Catalog file.

123 U.S. Labor Statistics Bureau. Di-

rectory of national and international labor unions in the United States. Govt. Print. Off., 1947– . Biennial. $1.25.

Issued as bulletins. Title varies. A good single title containing basic descriptive and statistical information pertaining to all aspects of unions.

124 U.S. Postal Service Postal service manual. Govt. Print. Off., 1970. Loose-leaf, with supplements for an indefinite period. Paper $25.

Contains the regulations governing the postal service; general operating rules, definitions and specifications of mailability, rates by class and distance, etc. Kept up-to-date by loose-leaf correction pages.

125 U.S. Post Office Department. Directory of international mail. Govt. Print. Off., 1955– . Irregular. 1v. $5 including binder; $2.50 without binder.

Rates governing mail to foreign countries, kept up to date with loose-leaf correction sheets.

126 ——— National zip code directory. Govt. Print. Off., 1967– . Annual. Paper $10.

Compilation of zip code numbers for all addresses in the United States. When a new volume is ready, the old one will be replaced by the Post Office at no charge.

127 World wide chamber of commerce directory. Johnson Publ., 1965– . Annually in July. Paper $4.

Lists chambers of commerce within and outside the United States (including foreign chambers of commerce with U.S. offices) and foreign embassies and government agencies located in the United States.

Dictionaries, Encyclopedias, and Handbooks

128 Aspley, John C. Sales manager's handbook. Ed. by Ovid Riso. 11th ed. Dartnell, 1968. 960p. $22.50.

A classic in the field; each edition adds much new information to assist the manager on sales organization, training, methods of selling, and marketing research. Explanation of trade practices is an important feature.

129 ——— Sales promotion handbook. 5th ed. Dartnell, 1966. 1000p. $22.50.

Almost a companion volume to *Sales Manager's Handbook;* this title emphasizes sales techniques and promotion ideas.

130 Business Abroad, *periodical.* World trade data yearbook. Donnelly, 1927– . $5.

Authoritative information on advertising, transportation, sales, marketing, and financial aspects of world trade. May issue of *Business Abroad.* Formerly January issue of *International Trade Review* published by Dun & Bradstreet. A new feature lists current trade fairs around the world.

131 Commodity yearbook. Commodity Research Bureau, 1939– . Annual. $18.95.

Background data and statistical history of more than 100 basic commodities and special commodity studies. A good quick-reference source.

132 Editor and publisher market guide. Editor and Publisher, 1924– . Annual. Paper $10.

Comprehensive data on daily newspaper markets, such as a city's population, location, trade areas, banks, climate, principal industries, colleges and universities, etc. Arranged by state and city.

133 International almanac of business and finance. Finance Publ., 1971– . Annual. $2.
Concise fiscal and economic data on foreign countries and the major U.S. corporations having branches abroad. Arranged by country. Index.

134 Frailey, Lester Eugene. Handbook of business letters. rev. ed. Prentice-Hall, 1965. 918p. $17.95.
A compendium of sample business letters designed to provide an appropriate model for every circumstance and contingency. Arranged by category. Index.

135 Frey, Albert W., ed. Marketing handbook. 2d ed. Ronald, 1965. 1292p. $17.50.
A guide for everyone concerned with selling and marketing goods and services. Modeled after the original *Marketing Handbook,* this book includes statistical and mathematical tools, laws of sales, and service policies, besides the usual marketing subjects.

136 Gross, Jerome S. Illustrated encyclopedic dictionary of real estate terms. Prentice-Hall, 1970. 468p. $16.
Provides readily understandable definitions and sample forms for the legal instruments used in real estate transactions.

137 Heyel, Carl. Encyclopedia of management. Reinhold, 1963. 1084p. $27.50.
Covers such topics as work simplification, retirement plans, and investment policy formulae. Arranged in dictio-

nary form with a definition and explanation of the topic, its history, a list of reference for further information and cross references.

138 Hutchinson, Lois. Standard handbook for secretaries. 8th ed. McGraw-Hill, 1969. 638p. $7.95.
The accepted basic title in the field. Index is particularly good because of its great detail. In addition to excellent office-practice information, the sections on English grammar, choice of words, and punctuation are invaluable. A table of installment payments and interest has been added.

139 Kohler, Eric Louis. Dictionary for accountants. 4th ed. Prentice-Hall, 1970. 456p. $17.95.
A standard work in the field, giving current definitions and information on more than 2700 terms in everyday language. Charts and forms where applicable.

140 Lasser, J. K. Handbook of accounting methods. 3d ed. Van Nostrand, 1964. 970p. $18.50.
Gives details of handling accounting problems in more than 60 different industries, with automatic data processing included where pertinent.

141 Munn, Glenn G. Encyclopedia of banking and finance. 6th ed. Bankers Publ., 1962. 788p. $25.
Primarily serves the banking, financial, and allied vocations with explanations and definitions of banking terms, but is still not too technical for the student. Alphabetically arranged. Bibliographies.

142 Office management handbook. Ed. by Harry L. Wylie; staff ed., James Q. Harty. 2d ed. Ronald, 1958. 890p. $14.

Developed under the auspices of the National Office Management Association, this is a comprehensive treatment of all the important aspects of office operations. Illustrations.

143 Sales Management, *periodical.* Survey of buying power. Sales Management. 1929– . Annual. $10.

Published as an issue of the periodical, this is one of the definitive surveys of population, effective buying income, and retail sales. Additional statistical estimates included.

144 Taintor, Sarah A., and Monro, K. M. Secretary's handbook: a manual of correct usage. 8th ed. Macmillan, 1958. 559p. $5.95.

Published since 1929, this has long been a classic handbook. Concentrates on problems of writing, with many examples of types of letters. Not quite so detailed on grammar as Hutchinson's *Standard Handbook for Secretaries.* A valuable title in the field.

145 U.S. President. Economic report of the President transmitted to the Congress. . . . Govt. Print. Off., 1947– . Annual. Paper $1.50.

An important document, not only for the up-to-date picture of the economy, but also for the invaluable statistical tables.

146 Writer's market. Writer's Digest, 1929– . Annual. $8.95.

Information on agents and markets for free-lance artists, photographers, and authors. A subject listing of special-interest markets from Astrology to Women's Magazines. Each listing includes name and address of the publication or company, its editorial needs, and its rate of payment. Additional lists of syndicates, writers' conferences, and writers' clubs are useful for the amateur author.

Insurance

147 Best's Key ratings guide: property-liability. Best, 1906– . Annual. $16.

Supplies quick-reference key ratings and comprehensive statistics showing the financial condition, general standing, and transactions of various types of insurance companies operating in the United States. Formerly called *Best's Insurance Guide with Key Ratings.*

148 Best's Insurance reports, life-health . . . upon legal reserve companies, fraternal benefit societies and assessment associations operating in the United States and Canada. Best, 1906– . Annual. $63.

Gives complete, up-to-date information concerning life insurance institutions.

Taxation

149 Commerce Clearing House. State tax handbook. The Clearing House, 1964– . Annual. $7.50.

Up-to-date information on types, forms, and rates of taxation operative within the various states. Information, in greatly condensed form, is extracted from CCH's *State Tax Guides.*

150 Lasser (J. K.) Institute. Your income tax. Simon & Schuster, 1937– . Annual. $1.95.

Designed to facilitate preparation of income-tax returns. Includes sample forms. Indexed.

151 U.S. Internal Revenue Service. Your federal income tax for individuals. Govt. Print. Off., 1944– . Annual. Paper 60¢

Useful booklet designed to help taxpayers prepare their tax returns. Simply written, it explains in detail what can and cannot be deducted, etc.

6 Social Sciences

Bibliographies and Indexes

152 Hoselitz, Bert F., ed. A reader's guide to the social sciences. Rev. ed. Free Pr., 1970. 425p. $8.95.

Essays, each written by a subject specialist, which explicate current trends and briefly survey the history of sociology, anthropology, psychology, political science, economics, and geography. Each essay cites the classical or landmark books of its discipline. General bibliography.

152a White, Carl M., ed. Sources of information in the social sciences. 2d ed. American Library Assn., 1973.

The first edition of this standard work (Bedminster Press, 1964) established its reputation as the leading source for the identification of both reference and substantive publications in the social science disciplines. ALA's second edition is a greatly augmented and updated revision, current as of late 1972.

153 Public Affairs Information Service. Bulletin. The Service, 1915– . Weekly; cumulated 5 times a yr. Weekly and cumulated bulletins and annual volume, $100; cumulated bulletins and annual volume, $50; annual volume, $25.

A subject index to periodicals, pamphlets, and government documents relating to the social sciences, public administration, and related topics.

Dictionaries and Encyclopedias

154 Encyclopedia of the social sciences. Ed. in chief, Edwin R. A. Seligman. Macmillan, 1937. 8v. $40 each; $195 the set.

In parts outdated but still a comprehensive encyclopedia of the whole field of the social sciences, prepared by top authorities in the fields. The new 17-volume *International Encyclopedia of the Social Sciences* does not supersede this set.

155 International encyclopedia of the social sciences. Collier-Macmillan, 1968. 17v. $495.

An important and valuable addition to this subject area. Originally planned as a new edition of the *Encyclopedia of the Social Sciences*, but, as completed, it is an entirely new work. Articles signed. Selected bibliographies and a comprehensive index are included.

156 Theodorson, George A. A modern dictionary of sociology. Crowell, 1969. 469p. $10.

Contains clear, succinct definitions of those sociological terms which modern readers are likely to encounter in books, textbooks, articles, and newspapers.

Directories

157 The foundation directory. 4th ed. The Foundation Center (distr. by Columbia Univ. Pr.), 1971. 642p. $15.

Lists 5,454 nongovernmental nonprofit foundations in the United States having assets of $500,000 or making annual grants totaling at least $25,000. Data elements covered for each include donor, purpose, assets, expenditures, and officers. Arranged by states. Three indexes: by fields of interest; donors, trustees and administrators; and foundation names.

158 Encyclopedia of associations. 7th ed. Gale, 1972. 2v. $25; 8 quarterly issues, 2-yr. subscription $48. v.1, National associations of the U.S. v.2, Geographic and executive indexes.

An indispensable directory of national associations. In classified order, gives for each entry such particulars as address, current officers, date of founding, purposes, and publications. Name and key word indexes in volume 1. Volume 2 indexes this material by location and officers. Volume 3 is the up-dating service.

Social Services

Directories

159 American Foundation for the Blind, Inc. Directory of agencies serving the visually handicapped in the United States. The Foundation, 1926– . Biennial $6.

A useful guide to state and local agencies. Also lists specialized agencies.

160 American Public Welfare Assn. Public welfare directory, 1970. The Association, 1970. 242p. $15.

A comprehensive list of federal, state, and local public assistance and welfare agencies, including officials. Material on "Where to write" for vital records. Not an annual, but correction notices issued frequently.

161 Greenberg, Dan. U.S. guide to nursing homes. Grosset, 1970. 3 v. $2.95 each. v.1, East Coast region, 160p. v.2, Midwest region, 203p. v.3, West Coast region, 148p.

Each volume is arranged by state and then by city. Provides basic data on: admissions policy, cost, medical care, dietary facilities, and safety and comfort services.

162 Hospitals, *periodical*. Hospitals: guide issue. American Hospital Assn., 1945– . Annual. $7.50.

Part 2 of the August issue of the periodical, *Hospitals,* contains a directory of registered hospitals and information on the American Hospital Assn., agencies, organizations, and educational programs. Gives detailed hospital statistics and a guide for hospital buyers.

163 National Assn. for Mental Health, Inc. Directory of facilities for mentally ill children in the United States, 1967. The Association, 1967. 178p. Paper $1.25.

This directory lists by state all available resources for mentally ill children. Each entry records the name of director, staffing pattern, fees, and other significant facets of these important services. Formerly entitled *Directory of Resources . . . .*

Minorities

Bibliographies

164 Johnson, Harry Alleyn, ed. Multi-

media materials for Afro-American studies: curriculum orientation and annotated bibliography of resources. Bowker, 1971. 353p. $19.95.

Part 1 consists of four position papers on black studies and the curriculum. The following two parts are devoted to classified listings of audiovisual materials.

165 Miller, Elizabeth W. The Negro in America: a bibliography. 2d ed. Harvard Univ. Pr., 1970. 351p. $10.

Containing 6500 entries for books, articles, and parts of books arranged in classified subject order. The best available bibliography in the field. Full author (but not subject) index.

166 Porter, Dorothy B., comp. The Negro in the United States: a selected bibliography. Library of Congress, 1970. 313p. $3.25.

A classified bibliography of predominantly recent monographs on the Negro in the Library of Congress. In addition it locates copies in eleven other research libraries. LC classification numbers. Author and subject index referring to serial entry numbers.

Encyclopedias and Handbooks

167 Adams, Russell. Great Negroes, past and present. Afro-American Publ., 1969. 3d ed. 212p. $6.95.

A classified biographical compendium of prominent Negroes in the U.S., Europe, and Africa. Sketches are illustrated. Bibliography. Index.

168 Davis, John Preston, ed. American Negro reference book. Prentice-Hall, 1966. 969p. $24.95.

Extensive and complete reference book on every major aspect of Negro life in America from colonial times to the present. Bibliographies and tables for most chapters. Well indexed.

169 Dennis, Henry C. American Indian, 1492–1970: a chronology and fact book. Foreword by Robert L. Bennett. Oceana, 1971. 137p. $5.

In addition to chronology, this work includes such elements as biographies of prominent Indians, past and present; tables; museums and organizations and audiovisual resources. Bibliography. Index.

170 Hodge, Frederick Webb. Handbook of American Indians north of Mexico. Scholarly Publ., 1968. 2v. $27.50. (Reprint of 1912 ed. issued by the Govt. Print. Off. as Bureau of American Ethnology. Bulletin no. 30)

An excellent encyclopedic survey providing specific subject access to all facets of American Indian cultures. Index.

171 Makers of America. Ed. by Wayne Moquin. Encyclopaedia Britannica Educational Corp., 1971. 10v. $79.50.

Beginning with the "Firstcomers" (v.1), proceeding through the "hyphenated Americans" (v.7) and concluding with "emergent minorities" this compilation of documents (extracts from published books, articles, government publications, manuscripts, etc.) depicts the ethnic pluralism of America. Structurally the work bears striking affinities to the publisher's companion compilation, the *Annals of America,* but is not, they insist, a "distillation" therefrom. Bibliography and five indexes by ethnic groups, proper names, topics, author-sources, and illustrations appear in volume 10.

172 Ploski, Harry A., and Kaiser, Ernest. Negro almanac: the Negro, his part in America. New rev. ed. Bellwether Publ., 1971. 1010p. $27.95.

Useful work arranged in 32 sections and covering four basic categories: history, the contemporary scene, statistical analysis, and biographical material. The last is particularly informative. Illustrations; bibliography; index.

Statistics

Bibliographies

173 Statistics sources: a guide to data on industrial, business, social, educational, financial and other topics for the United States and selected countries, ed. by Paul Wasserman, Eleanor Allen, and Charlotte Georgi. 3d ed. Gale, 1971. 647p. $27.50.

A compendium of terms and phrases under which are cited primary statistical sources. Cross references within text. Though most sources are U.S. produced, some UN sources provide limited international coverage.

Yearbooks

174 Almanack, by Joseph Whitaker. Whitaker (distr. in the United States by British Book Centre), 1869– . Annual. $6.50.

Similar to *World Almanac,* this annual contains an enormous amount of statistical and descriptive information concerning Great Britain, plus brief information for other parts of the world. Detailed index.

175 Chase's Calendar of annual events.

Apple Tree Pr., 1958– . Annual. $5.

Lists special days, weeks, and months.

176 Information please almanac. Simon & Schuster, 1947– . Annual. $3.95; paper $2.25.

Many facts assembled for quick reference. Needed even if *World Almanac* is purchased, for each volume contains some material not found in the other.

177 Guinness book of records. Sterling, 1955– . Annual. $4.95; library binding $6.39.

Title varies: some editions appear as *Guinness Book of World Records.*

A guide to the superlatives of the natural and human worlds; the first, the last, the tallest, the shortest, the most, and the least, etc. Arranged by broad topic. Detailed subject index.

178 New York Times encyclopedic almanac. New York Times Book and Educational Division, 1970– . Annual. $3.95.

Differs from other almanacs in that it draws on the full resources of the *New York Times.* Contains excellent news surveys in its "Times in depth" section.

179 Statesman's year-book: statistical and historical annual of the states of the world. Rev. after official returns. St. Martin's, 1864– . Annual. $13.50.

Excellent, concise yearbook giving detailed information concerning constitution and government, economic conditions, commerce, agriculture, religion, etc., of the governments of the world. Bibliographies of reference books for each country. Particularly good for Great Britain and members of the Commonwealth. Indexed.

180 United Nations. Statistical Office.
   Demographic yearbook. UN Publications (distr. by International
   Publications Service), 1949– .
   Annual. $19; paper $13.50.
Official compilation of international
demographic data in such fields as area
and population, natality, mortality,
marriage, divorce, international migra-
tion, etc. Each year some aspect of
demographic statistics is treated inten-
sively. The 1969 *Yearbook* discusses
"Natality Statistics." Many back volumes are still available.

181 World almanac and book of facts.
   Doubleday, 1868– . Annual.
   $3.95.
A ready-reference tool containing much
statistical material for the current and
preceding years, important events of
the year, associations, societies, and
their addresses, and many other items.
Indexed.

United States

182 U.S. Bureau of the Census. Census of population: 1970. Govt.
   Print. Off., 1971– .
The 19th decennial census is now being worked on. Presently available are
preliminary and advanced reports plus
final reports, in pamphlet form, for
"Number of Inhabitants" only. These
pamphlets come out by state at 35
cents and above. No bound volumes
have yet been published; each library
will want in the final bound set those
parts of volume 1, "Characteristics of
the Population," dealing with its own
state and possibly some adjoining states.
Pages and price vary with the size of
the state. A price list may be secured
from the Superintendent of Documents
without charge.

183 County and city data book, 1967.
   Govt. Print. Off., 1967. 673p.
   $7.75.
This volume provides, for convenient
reference, a selection of recent statistical information for counties, cities,
and other relatively small areas. Supplements the *Statistical Abstract*. A
new volume is prepared at intervals to
reflect latest census findings.

184 Historical statistics of the United
   States, colonial times to 1957.
   Govt. Print. Off., 1964. 789p.
   $8.25.
A valuable compilation of many important statistics taken from census records. This work supplies, for many
items, a retrospective record of data
formerly furnished in the *Statistical
Abstract*.

185 Historical statistics of the United
   States, colonial times to 1957.
   Continuation to 1962 and revisions. Govt. Print. Off., 1965.
   154p. $1.50.
For current U.S. statistics, see no. 186,
the one indispensable source.

186 Statistical abstract of the United
   States. Govt. Print. Off., 1879– .
   Annual. $5.75.
An indispensable collection of statistical data culled from the reports of
agencies of the United States. Usually
gives some retrospective statistics. Classified arrangement. Detailed index.

Politics and Government

Dictionaries

187 Plano, Jack Charles, and Greenberg, Milton. American political
   dictionary. Rev. and enl. ed. Holt,
   1967. 401p. $6.95.

The vocabulary of governmental institutions, practices, and traditions at the federal, state, and local levels.

Directories

188 Institute for the study of the U.S.S.R. Party and government officials of the Soviet Union, 1917–1967. Ed. by Edward L. Crowley. Scarecrow, 1969. 214p. $7.50.

Lists of members, with inclusive dates of tenure, of party and government organs. Arranged by party and government agency. General and name indexes.

Yearbooks

189 Political handbook and atlas of the world, governments and intergovernmental organizations. Publ. for the Council on Foreign Relations by Simon & Schuster, 1927– . Annual. $19.95; paper $4.95.

Data on chief government officials, political parties, their leaders and programs, political events, names of newspapers and their proprietors and editors, etc. A supplement which updates the parent volume appeared in 1971 under the title: *The World This Year* (Simon & Schuster, 1971– . Annual. $6.85).

United States

190 Barone, Michael, and others. The almanac of American politics. Gambit, 1972. 1030p. $12.95.

Provides essential data for the assessment of each Representative and Senator in the Congress. Specifics include political background on the state or Congressional district, biographies, voting records, group ratings (by such groups as Americans for Democratic Action and Americans for Constitutional Action) and recent election results. Arranged by state. Appendixes. Congressional district maps. Index.

191 Congressional Quarterly Service. Congress and the nation: a review of government and politics. The Service, 1965–69. 2v. $55 the set. v.1, 1945–1964 (1965), $27.50; v.2, 1965–1968 (1969), $33.

Comprehensive surveys of the interactions of national issues in all fields of social concern and congressional legislation. Arranged under broad topics such as economic policy, labor, agriculture, etc. Indexes.

192 Congressional Quarterly Service. Weekly report. 1945– . The Service, $144 (includes bound almanac)

Succinct reporting source on the week in Congress: new bills, progress of pending bills, summaries of legislation of the year and session to date. Special articles. Index.

193 Porter, Kirk H., and Johnson, Donald Bruce, comps. National party platforms, 1840–1968. 4th ed. Univ. of Illinois Pr., 1970. 723p. $13.50.

Texts of the platforms of major and minor parties are included in this collection, which includes the first of these important political statements.

194 U.S. Bureau of the Budget. Budget in brief. Govt. Print. Off., 1950– . Annual. Paper 40¢

In addition to this summary of the federal budget, every library should have copies of its state and local budgets, or at least abstracts of them, for the current year.

195 U.S. Bureau of the Census. Congressional district atlas: 86th Congress. Govt. Print. Off., 1960– . Biennial. $1.75.

Consists of maps showing the boundaries of congressional districts. Arranged by states. Counties are keyed to districts.

196 U.S. Laws, statutes, etc. U.S. code. 1964 ed. containing the general and permanent laws of the United States in force on January 3, 1965. Prepared and published . . . by the Committee on the Judiciary of the House of Representatives. Govt. Print. Off., 1964. 14v. $87.25 the set.

Although the medium-sized library cannot satisfy all the needs of the legal specialist, it is important to supply the codified laws of the United States.

197 U.S. President. Inaugural addresses of the Presidents of the United States from George Washington, 1789, to Richard Milhous Nixon, 1969. Comp. by the Library of Congress Legislative Reference Service. Govt. Print. Off., 1969. 279p. Paper $1.50.

An illuminating compilation, indicating the initial professions of political ideology with which each presidential term began its experiment in government.

198 Wynar, Lubomyr R. American political parties: a selective guide to parties and movements of the 20th century. Libraries Unlimited, 1969. 427p. $13.50.

A bibliography of periodical articles, books and dissertations on major and minor political parties in the United States. Two brief chapters on Ameri-

can government and history are appended. Index.

DIRECTORIES

199 Book of the states. Council of State Governments, 1935– . Biennial. $12.50; with two supplements $16.

In addition to general articles on various aspects of state government, provides many statistical and directory data, and the nickname, motto, flower, bird, song, and chief officials of each state. The supplements list latest elective officials and legislators.

200 Congressional Quarterly Service. Members of Congress, 1945–1970. The Service, 1971. 44p. $2.50.

Names, birthdates, and years of congressional service. Supplementary listings of congressional leaders, committee chairmen, etc.

201 Congressional Quarterly Service. Congressional Quarterly's guide to the Congress of the United States, origins, history, and procedure. The Service, 1971. 983p. $35.

A complete guide to the intelligent study of the Congress in all of its phases. Special features include, among many others, glossaries of terms, bibliographies, a biographical directory of Congress, texts of basic documents, standing rules of the House and Senate. Full subject index.

202 Congressional staff directory. 13th ed., 1971. 713p. $13.50.

Brief biographies of Congressmen and Senators, their committee assignments, and biographies of their staff members. A list of Congressmen representing each city in the country arranged by state. Index.

203 Municipal year book: an authoritative résumé of activities and statistical data of American cities. International City Management Assn., 1934– . Annual. $15.
Very complete statistical data, combined with current information on individual city programs, urban counties, and metropolitan areas. Includes directory of city officials and bibliographies for major areas of urban affairs.

204 U.S. Congress. Official Congressional directory for the use of the U.S. Congress. Govt. Print. Off., 1809– . Annual. $4; thumb-indexed $5.50.
Complete listing of organization and members of Congress, including biographical sketches, Congressional committees, commissions; boards, and departments; also information on the judiciary, diplomats and consular service, press and other galleries, and small maps showing congressional districts. Indexed.

205 United States government organization manual. Govt. Print. Off., 1935– . Annual. Paper $3.
Most important annually revised source of information on all government agencies, giving history, organization authority, activities, and chief officials with organizational charts. Also lists agencies abolished, transferred, and terminated. Index of names as well as general index.

CONSTITUTION

206 Constitution of the United States of America, analysis and interpretation. Govt. Print. Off., 1964. 1693p. $15.50.
Contains annotations of Supreme Court decisions through June 22, 1964, and provides the current operative meaning of all articles of the Constitution.

207 Cushman, Robert Eugene, and Cushman, Robert F. Cases in constitutional law. 3d. ed. rev. and enl. Appleton, 1968. 1186p. $11.50.
A comprehensive collection of important Supreme Court decisions, for the student of American constitutional law. Each case is preceded by an explanatory comment. Updated by pocket supplements.

208 Cushman, Robert Eugene. Leading constitutional decisions. 14th ed. Appleton. 1971 700p. Paper $4.75.
A collection of the most important Supreme Court decisions on constitutional questions of lasting importance through the fall of 1962. For the use of students of American government and history.

LAW

209 Ballentine, James Arthur. Ballentine's Law dictionary with pronunciations. 3d ed. Lawyers' Co-operative, 1969. 1429p. $30.
A standard dictionary which strikes a judicious balance between the inherent complexity of the law and simplification for laymen. Eminently suitable for the nonlaw library.

210 Kling, Samuel G. Complete guide to everyday law. 2d ed. Follett, 1970. 625p. $7.95.
A layman's guide to basic legal questions covering marriage, wills, contracts, legal forms, lawyer's fees, and many other important topics in clear question-and-answer method. This completely revised edition presents new material on social security, veterans' benefits, civil rights, and divorce.

211 Landau, Norman J., and Rheingold, Paul D. Introduction by Ralph Nader. Friends of the earth: an environmental law handbook. Ballantine, 1971. 496p. Paper $1.25.

A practical guide to the aroused citizen's legal attack on pollution problems, from investigating methods to preparation of court cases. Glossary of terms and bibliography.

212 American Bar Association. Committee on Business Law Libraries. Recommended law books. Ed. by Richard Sloane. The Association, 1969. 307p. $5.

An excellent working list of basic law books for lawyers and for law collections in general libraries. Classified, annotated. No index but a detailed table of contents.

213 The Time-Life family legal guide: what you need to know about the law. Time-Life Books, 1971. 400p. $11.95.

An up-to-date guide to the interpretation of law, intelligently written in language which is neither too technical nor unduly condescending. Bibliography. Index.

Parliamentary Procedure

214 Robert, Henry Martyn. Robert's Rules of order, newly revised. New and enl. ed. by Sarah Corbin Robert and others. Scott, Foresman, 1970. 594p. $5.95.

A compendium of parliamentary law, explaining methods of organizing and conducting the business of societies, conventions, and other assemblies. The 1970 edition, the first major revision since 1915, supersedes all previous editions. Among the many changes in this rewritten work are new charts, updated information, elimination of obsolete material, and the grouping of all material into chapters.

International Relations

215 Annuaire des organisations internationales. Yearbook of international organizations. Union of International Organizations (distr. in U.S. by International Publications Service), 1948– . Biennial. $28.

An encyclopedic dictionary of international organizations and associations currently active; their functions, officers, their abbreviations, aims, finance, activities, and publications.

216 Everyman's United Nations, a complete handbook of the activities and evolution of the United Nations during its first twenty years, 1945–1965. 8th ed. United Nations Office of Public Information, 1968. 634p. Paper $2.50.

A first purchase for general information about the United Nations.

217 Plano, Jack C., and Olten, Roy. International relations dictionary. Holt, 1969. 337p. $3.95.

A succinct handbook of current terms arranged in 12 topical chapters with a detailed subject index. Topical arrangement affords a contextual analysis; index provides access to particular terms.

218 Treaties and alliances of the world: a survey of international treaties in force and communities of states. Keesing's Publications Ltd. in collaboration with Scribner's, 1968. 158p. $13.50.

This survey summarizes the main provisions of international treaties and agreements in force as of March 1, 1968. Always indicates signatory powers and cites page references in *Keesing's Contemporary Archives* where full texts may be found.

219 United Nations. Yearbook. Columbia Univ. Pr. in cooperation with the United Nations, 1946/47– . Annual. $25.

An annual summary of the activities of the UN's constituent bodies and specialized agencies. Subject and name indexes.

Etiquette

220 Post, Emily (Price). Etiquette: the blue book of social usage. 12th ed. Funk (distr. by Crowell), 1969. 721p. $7.95.

Although Vanderbilt's *New Complete Book of Etiquette* covers every topic in manners and social behavior, "Emily Post" is still in demand; especially for formal occasions. Both volumes are recommended for all libraries.

221 Vanderbilt, Amy. New complete book of etiquette: the guide to gracious living. New rev. ed. Doubleday, 1963. 738p. $5.95; thumb-indexed $6.95.

Well adapted to the fashions and customs of modern life. It covers in detail every facet of social behavior and manners in today's world.

Holidays

222 Douglas, George William. American book of days: a compendium of information about holidays, festivals, notable anniversaries and Christian and Jewish holy days, with notes on other American anniversaries worthy of remembrance. 2d ed. rev. by Helen Douglas Compton. Wilson, 1948. 697p. $8.

Descriptive account of important days in secular and religious life. Chronological arrangement.

223 Gaster, Theodore Herzl. Festivals of the Jewish year. Peter Smith, 1962. 308p. $4.25. (Reprint of 1953 Sloane ed.)

The major Jewish festivals analyzed historically and compared with corresponding rites and customs of other religious traditions. Bibliography.

224 Hazeltine, Mary Emogene. Anniversaries and holidays: a calendar of days and how to observe them. 2d ed. comp. rev. with the editorial assistance of Judith K. Sollenberger. American Library Assn., 1944. 316p. $7.

Although this book is now twenty years old, it affords a comprehensive record of important dates in calendar-year order. Includes many bibliographical references.

225 Spicer, Dorothy G. Book of festivals. Gale, 1969. 429p. $12.50 (Reprint of 1937 ed.)

The standard work surveying festivals of all religious traditions.

226 Spicer, Dorothy Gladys. Festivals of Western Europe. Wilson, 1958. 275p. $5.

Descriptive material on the principal festivals of Belgium, Denmark, France, Germany, Italy, Luxembourg, The Netherlands, Norway, Portugal, Spain, Sweden, and Switzerland. Contains a table of Easter dates and movable festivals dependent upon Easter, 1958–87 inclusive; a glossary of festival terms; bibliography; and indexes of festivals by name and by country.

7 Education

Dictionaries and Encyclopedias

227 Encyclopedia of education. Macmillan & Free Pr., 1971. 10v. $395.

Designed as a complete encyclopedia of educational practice as reflected in institutions, processes and products. More than 1,000 articles, signed and equipped with bibliographies. Volume 10 comprises the index to the set.

228 Encyclopedia of educational research: a project of the American Educational Research Association. Ed. by Chester W. Harris. 3d ed. Macmillan, 1960. 1564p. $27.50.

Summarizes and critically evaluates reported research in many areas of education. Each topic includes a bibliography. More recent research may be followed in the *Review of Educational Research,* a periodical published under the same auspices.

229 Good, Carter Victor, ed. Dictionary of education. 2d ed. McGraw-Hill, 1959. 676p. $12.95.

A comprehensive dictionary of technical and professional terms and concepts. Excludes names of persons, institutions, school systems, and places except when a movement, method, or plan is represented. Includes foreign educational terms most frequently employed in the study of comparative education. Pro-

nunciation is given for difficult and foreign language words and for medical and psychological terms.

Directories

230 American Council on Education. American colleges and universities. Ed. by Otis Singletary. 10th ed. The Council, 1968. 1782p. $22.

An encyclopedic work on higher education, usually revised every four years. Part 1 gives an overview of the field: college admissions, history and structure of higher education, relationship to the federal government and foreign student in the United States. Part 2 covers professional education. Part 3, the main part, lists colleges and universities by state. For each it includes type, history, entrance requirements, fees, departments and staff, distinctive programs and activities, degrees, enrollment, foreign students, library, publications, student aid, finances, buildings and grounds, and administrative officers. Appendixes provide information on accreditation, academic costume, degree abbreviations, earned doctorates conferred 1861–1966, and ROTC units. Indexed.

231 American junior colleges. 7th ed. Ed. by Edmund J. Gleazer, Jr. American Council on Education, 1967. 957p. $14.

Information on 751 accredited junior colleges, usually revised every four years. Pattern is similar to that of *American Universities and Colleges,* to which this book is a companion volume. In addition to all the usual data, it includes each college's programs of study for transfer to senior colleges, as well as those for terminal or vocational-technical courses. Appendixes include information on regional accrediting agencies, off-campus housing, curricula, admission, church-related colleges, and changes since 6th edition.

232 A guide to graduate study: programs leading to the Ph.D. degree. Ed. by Robert Quick. 4th ed. American Council on Education, 1969. 637p. $15.

The standard guide to graduate programs. Arranged alphabetically by institution. Indexes.

233 Baird, William R. Baird's Manual of American college fraternities. 18th ed. Banta. 1968. 891p. $9.

Histories, including chapter lists of undergraduate and professional-school fraternities and honor societies. Also lists campuses and their fraternities.

234 Cass, James, and Birnbaum, Max. Comparative guide to American colleges for students, parents, and counselors. 4th ed. Harper, 1969. 837p. $10, paper $4.95.

Differs from most college directories by giving a profile of each institution, including academic atmosphere of campus and percent of applicants admitted. Its Selectivity Index ranks institutions by the academic potential of their student bodies. Also contains a list of public institutions that accept out-of-state students, and a list of institutions conferring the largest number of degrees in selected fields.

235 College handbook. College Entrance Examination Board, 1941– . Biennial. 1327p. Paper $4.75 (1969).

Limited to member institutions of the College Entrance Examination Board, all of which are fully accredited. Includes basic information such as location, size, programs of study, terms of admission, annual expenses, financial aid, and where to write for further information.

236 Directory for exceptional children. Ed. by D. R. Young. 6th ed. Sargent, 1969. 1152p. $12.

Designed to encompass all facilities for training, rehabilitation, therapy, and education of children unacceptable to, or unable to benefit fully from, regular schools. Answers queries of doctors, social workers, counselors, and parents. Excludes programs for the gifted.

237 Early childhood education directory. Bowker, 1971– . Irregular. $15.

A directory of pre-kindergarten educational centers in the United States. Arranged alphabetically by state and then city. Entries include all pertinent data such as history, calender, admissions policy, curriculum, facilities. Index.

238 Educators guide to free films. Educators Progress Service, 1941– . Annual. Paper $10.75.

Alphabetical listing of free films under each of 24 curriculum areas. Entries include technical description, annotation, and source. Separate indexes for titles, subjects, and sources.

239 Educators guide to free filmstrips.

37

Educators Progress Service, 1949– . Annual. Paper $8.50.

Similar in format to *Educators Guide to Free Films.*

240 American Council on Education. Accredited institutions of higher education. The Council, 1964– . Annual. $2.50.

Published for the Federation of Regional Accrediting Commissions of Higher Education. Arranged alphabetically by state. Entries include name of institution, statement of control, dates of first regional accreditation, degrees offered, officers and latest fall enrollment. Part 2 contains long descriptions of institutions accredited since the latest editions of *American Colleges and Universities* and *American Junior Colleges.*

241 Barron's Profiles of American colleges. Barron's Educational Service, 1964– . Irregular. $9.95; paper $4.95 (1971–72 ed.)

Arranged by state and then alphabetically by institution, entries provide the following data in standardized format. Student life, programs of study, expenses, admissions and admissions procedures. Index.

242 Guide to summer camps and summer schools. 17th ed. Porter Sargent, 1971. 474p. $5.

Includes academic as well as summer travel and camping programs. Entries indicate levels of skill needed and cost. Arranged by interest categories. Index.

243 Handbook of private schools, an annual descriptive survey of independent education. Sargent, 1915– . Annual. $14.

Long recognized as the principal directory of private schools. Gives the following data, for both boarding and day schools: type, location, director, admissions officer, curriculum, date established, school calendar, admissions, enrollment, faculty, graduates, tuition, summer session, plant evaluation, endowment, establishment and calendar, and association membership. Also discusses tutorial and remedial schools.

244 Livesey, Herbert, and Robbins, Gene A. Guide to American graduate schools. 2d ed. Viking, 1970. $12.95.

Describes graduate programs in 600 universities, arranged alphabetically. Indexes by subject fields and by geographic locations.

245 Lovejoy's College guide. 11th ed. Simon & Schuster, 1970. 447p. $7.50; paper $3.95.

The most asked-for guide to colleges. Part 1 is an orientation for parents and prospective students to virtually all aspects of college: costs, admissions, religious affiliations, and activities, etc. Part 2 explains accreditation and symbols used to classify colleges, lists colleges according to career curricula, and provides rating and description of institutions which form the major part of the guide. Now revised biennially. A monthly *Lovejoy's Guidance Digest* is published to bridge the gaps between revisions of the *Guide.*

246 Lovejoy's Scholarship guide. Rev. ed. Simon & Schuster, 1964. 91p. $4.95; paper $2.95.

Guide to scholarships, loans, and part-time jobs. Simpler and less detailed than Feingold.

247 Patterson's American education. Educational Directories, Inc., 1904– . Annual. $25.

A comprehensive directory of educational institutions: state departments of education, public school systems, private and denominational schools, special schools, colleges, and universities. Arranged by state, then by town, and by classification of specialty. Also includes educational associations and societies, lists of superintendents, and index.

248 Roose, Kenneth D., and Anderson, Charles J. A rating of graduate programs. American Council on Education, 1970. 115p. Paper $4.

Arranged by field of study, this study ranks the effectiveness of graduate programs with reference to the quality of their component faculties. Its purpose is to record changes in status since the publication of: Allan Murray Cartter, *An Assessment of Quality in Graduate Education* (American Council on Education, 1966. 131p. $5, paper $3). For maximum return, the two studies should be used conjointly.

249 Study abroad: international scholarships and courses. (distr. in U.S. by Unipub. Inc.) UNESCO, 1948– . Biennial. Paper $6.

Information on opportunities for study, research, and educational travel abroad at the university level. "As part of UNESCO's contribution to the observance of International Education Year, the present edition gives details of international courses . . . available to students whether or not financial assistance has been provided." "Vacation Study Abroad" has been eliminated from this issue, but similar information will be contained in a separate publication. Companion volume is UNESCO *Handbook of International Exchange,* which gives information on more than 5,300 agencies and organizations conducting programs of international exchange and cultural cooperation. Arranged by field of study, type of program, and country.

▶ Formerly the publications described in nos. 250–53 were all parts of the *Education Directory.* (Part 5, *Federal Governments,* has been eliminated.) By the time of the 1970–71 directories, it is planned that they will all be separate, no longer designated as parts, and be published by the National Center for Educational Statistics.

250 U.S. Office of Education. Education directory. Pt. 1, State governments, 1969–1970. Govt. Print. Off., 1969. 163p. Paper $1.

Covers 50 states and outlying areas. Lists principal officers of state agencies responsible for elementary and secondary education and vocational-technical education in the United States.

251 —— Education directory. Pt. 2, Public school systems, elementary and secondary education, 1969–1970. Govt. Print. Off., 1970. 313p. Paper $2.50.

252 National Center for Educational Statistics. Education directory: higher education, 1969–1970. Govt. Print. Off., 1970. 529p. Paper $4.50.

Any school with at least a two-year college program in residence is listed, with telephone, address, enrollment, calendar, affiliation, etc. Formerly part 3 of the *Education Directory* and issued by the U.S. Office of Education.

253 U.S. Office of Education. Education directory. Pt. 4, Education associations, 1969–1970. Govt.

Print. Off., 1970. 109p. Paper $1.25.

254 World of learning. Europa Publications (distr. in U.S. by Gale and the British Book Centre), 1947– . Annual. $42.

The standard international directory for the nations of the world, covering learned societies, research institutes, libraries, museums and art galleries, universities and colleges. Includes for each institution: address, officers, purpose, foundation date, publications, etc. Index.

Handbooks

255 Proia, Nicholas, and Di Gaspari, Vincent M. Barron's Handbook of American college financial aid. Barron, 1971. 701p. $6.95.

Arranged by state and then alphabetically by institution. Covers scholarships, loans, deferred tuition grants, work-study programs, etc. Detailed, up-to-date information. Index.

256 Institute for International Study. Handbook on international study for U.S. nationals. The Institute, 1955– . Triennial. $7.

Describes educational programs in foreign countries, exchange arrangements and summer opportunities. Bibliography. Index.

257 U.S. Office of Education. Digest of educational statistics. Govt. Print. Off., 1962– . Annual. $1.50.

Statistical summary of public and private elementary, secondary, and higher education in the United States. Federal programs and vocational education are also noted. Contains many useful tables and an index.

258 Woellner, Elizabeth H., and Wood, M. Aurilla. Requirements for certification of teachers, counselors, librarians, and administrators for elementary schools, secondary schools, junior colleges. Univ. of Chicago Pr., 1935– . Annual. Paper $7.85 (1971–72).

Provides detailed minimum requirements for certification by semester hours. Arrangement is by state. Important to have latest edition.

Vocations

259 Angel, Juvenal. Why and how to prepare an effective job résumé. 4th ed. World Trade Academy Pr., 1965. 250p. $9.

A complete guide to the preparation of job résumés. Based on an examination of 10,000 résumés, the work provides samples for all professional and technical occupations.

260 Directory of overseas summer jobs. Vacation-work (distr. in U.S. by National Directory Service), 1969– . Annual. $4.95.

Designed to provide details on full-time summer jobs available outside the United States. Arranged by country. Entries cover job descriptions, eligibility requirements, remuneration, and addresses for applications.

261 Lovejoy's Career and vocational guide; a source book, clue book and directory of job training opportunities. 3d enl. and compl. rev. ed. Simon & Schuster, 1967. 176p. $6.50; paper $3.95.

A comprehensive guide to the expanding field of vocational education, including a detailed listing of training programs in the armed services, apprenticeship programs, and home-study courses. Directory section includes schools which offer training in trades and technologies, airline jobs, medical and health services, performing arts, etc. All schools listed were resurveyed for this edition.

262 Blue book of occupational education. CCM Information Corp., 1971. 897p. $29.95.

Comprehensive guide to occupational schools of the United States, arranged by state and city. Includes a detailed index by curricula and programs of instructions. Additional sections cover such topics as financial and apprenticeships, and guides to job openings.

263 Summer employment directory. National Directory Service, 1952– . Annual. $5.95.

Lists employment openings for high school and college students, teachers and foreign students by state.

264 U.S. Bureau of Labor Statistics. Occupational outlook handbook. U.S. Govt. Print. Off., 1949– . Biennial. $6.25.

Trends and prospects for all major occupations. Provides particulars on potential earnings, qualifications, working conditions and further information sources. A standard source. Index.

265 U.S. Employment Service. Dictionary of occupational titles. 3d ed. Govt. Print. Off., 1965. 2v. v.1, $5; v.2, $4.25.

The standard codification of definitions and classifications of occupational titles in the United States, used both in the federal government and throughout the private sector. Volume 1 contains definitions and volume 2 the classification and industry codes. For those who must relate the third to the second edition the following is indispensable.

265a ——— Conversion table of code and title changes between the second and third editions. Govt. Print. Off., 1965. 1044p. $5.50.

8 Science and Technology

Bibliographies and Indexes

266 Applied science and technology index. Wilson, 1958– . Monthly except Aug. Annual cumulations. Service basis.

An index, by subject only, to approximately 225 periodicals in the fields of aeronautics, automation, chemistry, construction, electricity and electronics, engineering, geology and metallurgy, industrial and mechanical arts, machinery, physics, telecommunication, transportation, and related areas. Established in 1958 when *Industrial Arts Index* was divided into two separate indexes: *Applied Science and Technology Index* and *Business Periodicals Index*.

267 Biological and agricultural index. Wilson, 1964– . Monthly except Aug. Annual cumulations. Service basis. In print: v.12 (1948) through v.23 (1969).

Called the *Agricultural Index* prior to 1964. A detailed alphabetical subject index to agricultural, biological, and related periodicals in the English language.

Directories

268 Scientific and technical societies of the United States. 8th ed. National Academy of Sciences, 1968. 221p. $12.50.

Lists addresses, names of officers, history, purpose, professional activities, number of members, titles of publications, and number of meetings a year for each society. With this edition such societies as trade associations, undergraduate groups, and fund raising organizations have been eliminated. Furthermore, the Canadian Council is now publishing its own list rather than be included here as in previous editions. An annual supplement will update names and addresses.

Dictionaries, Encyclopedias, and Handbooks

269 Crispin, Frederic Swing. Dictionary of technical terms: containing definitions of commonly used expressions in aeronautics, architecture, woodworking and building trades, electrical and metalworking trades, printing, chemistry, plastics, etc. 11th ed. rev. Bruce, 1970. 455p. $6.95.

Intended for students, draftsmen, technicians, mechanics, and others engaged in practical technical work. About 10,000 terms defined briefly, i.e., in one or two lines. Includes pronunciation.

270 Harper encyclopedia of science. Ed. by James R. Newman. rev. ed. Harper, 1967. 2v. 1379p. $40; lib. ed. $32.95.

A useful science encyclopedia for the

layman. Contains nearly 4,000 signed articles on the physical sciences, mathematics, biology, logic, and the history and philosophy of science. Extensive index, biographies, numerous illustrations, and a classified bibliography. The 1967 edition contains the text of the four-volume 1963 edition with some changes and new articles.

271 McGraw-Hill encyclopedia of science and technology: an international reference work. 3d ed. rev. and enl. McGraw-Hill, 1971. 15v. $295 to schools and libraries.
Useful for all levels of readers and in all types of libraries where there is need for authoritative, well-written, clearly explained, and fully illustrated scientific-technical information. Represented are all the natural sciences and all their major applications in agriculture, engineering, forestry, and food technologies, etc. but not in psychiatry or clinical medicine.

272 Annual supplement: McGraw-Hill yearbook of science and technology, 1962– . $24.
The 1970 yearbook is the last to be published in this format. Subsequent volumes will follow the style of the third edition of the *McGraw-Hill Encyclopedia of Science and Technology.* This edition has a cumulative index to the volumes 1966–70.

273 The way things work: an illustrated encyclopedia of technology. Simon & Schuster, 1967–71. 2v. $9.95 each.
A practical guide to machines and processes which in every instance explains how things work. Fully illustrated. Arranged in classified order. Indexes.

Natural Sciences

Astronomy

274 Rudaux, Lucien, and Vaucouleurs, G. de. Larousse encyclopedia of astronomy. 2d ed. Putnam, 1959. 506p. $17.
An excellent encyclopedic introduction to astronomy. Lavishly illustrated. Classified treatment of material. Index.

275 Menzel, Donald Howard. Field guide to the stars and planets, including the moon, satellites, comets, and other features of the universe. Houghton, 1964. 397p. $5.95.
A useful handbook for both the layman and the professional astronomer. Clearly written, well illustrated, with a glossary of astronomical terms and adequate index.

276 Moore, Patrick. Atlas of the universe. Foreword by Sir Bernard Lovell. Rand McNally, 1970. 272p. $35.
A highly successful popular presentation of the moon, the solar system and the stars in approximately 1500 photographs most of which are in color. Index.

Climatology

277 U.S. Environmental Data Service. Climatic atlas of the United States. Govt. Print. Off., 1968. 80p. $4.25.
Climatic maps showing temperature patterns, winds, humidity, precipitation, etc.

Biology

278 Altman, Philip L., and Dittmer, Dorothy S., eds. Biological data

book. Federation of American Societies for Experimental Biology, 1972. 3v. $30 each; $75 the set.

A basic reference for biology, organized into quantitative and descriptive tables, charts, and diagrams. Many citations to standard authorities.

279 Gray, Peter. Dictionary of the biological sciences. Reinhold, 1967. 602p. $14.75.

A primary reference source for the vocabulary of the entire spectrum of the life sciences. Reliable and authoritative.

280 ———, ed. Encyclopedia of the biological sciences. 2d ed. Van Nostrand Reinhold, 1970. 1027p. $24.95.

More than 800 signed articles written by specialists, covering the developmental, ecological, functional, genetic, structural, and taxonomic aspects of the biological sciences. Long, detailed articles not only define, explain, and describe their subject, but also offer additional reference sources. A well-designed reference tool for a broad audience ranging from the high school biology student to the practicing biologist. Adequately illustrated. Indexed.

Botany

281 House, Homer Doliver. Wildflowers: three hundred and sixty-four full color illustrations with complete descriptive text. Macmillan, 1961. 362p. $17.95 (Reprint of 1935 ed.)

The wildflowers of the United States, lovingly described and beautifully illustrated. A full color illustration for most flowers. Introductory material on basic botany. List of illustrations. Index by both popular and scientific names.

282 Petrides, George A. Field guide to trees and shrubs: field marks of all trees, shrubs, and woody vines that grow wild in the Northeastern and North-Central United States and in southeastern and south-central Canada. Houghton, 1958. 431p. $5.95.

An adequate guide to the trees, shrubs, and vines of the Northeast.

Chemistry and Physics

283 Besançon, Robert M., ed. The encyclopedia of physics. Van Nostrand, 1968. 832p. $25.

Especially useful for those who need explanations of physical concepts encountered in the pursuit of professions and interests other than physics.

284 Clark, George L., and Hawley, Gessner G., eds. Encyclopedia of chemistry. 2d ed., Reinhold, 1966. 1144p. $27.50.

This unique one-volume encyclopedia covers the field of chemical knowledge with a surprising degree of depth. Approximately one third of the articles are new to this edition, and most of the remainder have been thoroughly revised. However, articles dealing with famous chemists and institutions have been reluctantly dropped. A 30-page index with about 5000 entries facilitates location of information not readily found in the alphabetized contents.

285 Condensed chemical dictionary. 8th ed. Rev. by Gessner G. Hawley. Van Nostrand Reinhold, 1971. 1044p. $27.50.

Defines principal terms and concisely describes commercial and trademarked chemical products. Terminology reflecting the advances in thermonuclear phenomena has been added. Also serves as an excellent source of information about official pharmaceuticals and drugs.

286 Condon, Edward Uhler, and Odishaw, Hugh, eds. Handbook of physics. 2d ed. McGraw-Hill, 1967. Unpaged. $34.75.

A brave attempt to condense the whole of physics into one volume. Emphasizes theory and omits experimental methods and data. Bibliography for each of the articles.

287 Handbook of chemistry and physics: a ready-reference book of chemical and physical data. Chemical Rubber Co, 1913– . Annual. $25.75.

A compilation of essential tables of physical and chemical properties of elements and compounds.

Geology

288 Challinor, John. Dictionary of geology. 3d ed. Oxford Univ. Pr., 1967. 298p. $7.

A more than adequate work which defines terms and examines meanings and concepts. Selected quotations and references support most entries.

289 Pough, Frederick H. Field guide to rocks and minerals. 3d ed. Houghton, 1960. 349p. $5.95.

An excellent handbook for identification purposes. Photographs of rocks and minerals are accompanied by a diagrammatic sketch of the crystal shape of the mineral and a description of its physical properties, composition, identification tests, and distinguishing characteristics.

290 Ransom, Jay E. Fossils in America: their nature, origin, identification, and classification and a range guide to collecting sites. Harper, 1964. 402p. $8.95.

Elementary background materials on fossil collection and identification, field geology, and map reading are outlined. More than half the book is an alphabetical directory of fossil-hunting spots; places are arranged by state, county, township, and sections providing species or genera of collectible fossils. For fossil hunters and beginning paleontologists. Lists libraries and mineral museums in the United States.

291 Shipley, Robert Morrill, assisted by Beckley, Anna McConnell, and others. Dictionary of gems and gemology including ornamental, decorative, and curio stones: a glossary of over 4000 English and foreign words, terms, and abbreviations which may be encountered in English literature on the gem, jewelry, or art trades. 5th ed. Gemological Institute of America, 1951. 261p. $5.50.

Includes historical matter and pronunciation. Reference is occasionally made to authority supplying specific information, with an additional entry under the authority.

292 Webster, R. A. Gems, their sources, descriptions, and identification. 2d ed. Archon, 1970. 836p. $45.

A landmark work on precious stones by a gemologist who is able to describe both the materials and the instruments by which they are studied. Also deals with technical aspects and the various methods of gem identification. Color plates and extensive identification tables. Bibliography.

Mathematics

293 Barlow, Peter. Barlow's Tables of squares, cubes, square roots, cube roots, and reciprocals of all integer numbers up to 12,500. Ed. by L. J. Comrie. 4th ed. Chapman and Hall (distr. by Barnes & Noble), 1965 (c1941). 258p. $4.95; paper $3.25.

Highly utilitarian compilations, valuable to laymen and scientists alike. Exceptionally accurate.

294 James, Glenn, and James, Robert Clarke, eds. Mathematics dictionary. Multilingual ed. Van Nostrand Reinhold, 1968. 517p. $17.50.

A correlated condensation of mathematical concepts designed to serve the needs of both students and scholars. Format suitable for highspeed reference work. Multilingual index.

295 Jansson, Martin Ernest. Handbook of applied mathematics, ed. by Edward E. Grazda, Morris Brenner, and William R. Minrath. 4th ed. Van Nostrand, 1966. 1119p. $11.50.

Covers succinctly the main principles of mathematics and then in subsequent chapters explains how these underlie the operations of the practical arts and sciences, e.g. carpentry, plumbing, electricity. Index.

296 Minrath, William R. Handbook of business mathematics. 2d ed. Van Nostrand, 1967. 658p. $9.85.

Exhibits a tripartite organization: basic mathematical concepts, methods of business mathematics, and specific applications. The second edition contains a wealth of material on computers and their industrial and commercial applications. Index.

297 Naft, Stephen. International conversion tables. Expanded and rev. by Ralph DeSola. Hawthorn, 1966. 372p. $7.95.

Accurate and handy ready-reference source for persons in international commerce, science, and management occupations. Authority is U.S. Bureau of Standards to the extent that U.S. standards are available.

298 Ronnigen Metric Co. Weights and measures: U.S. to metric, metric to U.S., prepared by Helmer A. Ronnigen. The Company, 1969. 74p. $6.75.

As the United States prepares to change over to the metric system, these conversion tables will assume increasing importance.

Zoology

299 American Kennel Club. Complete dog book. Rev. ed. Doubleday, 1968. 580p. $6.

Treats the care, feeding, diseases, selection, and handling of purebred dogs, plus a wealth of other information.

300 Axelrod, Herbert R. Exotic tropical fishes. TFH Publications (distr. by Sterling), 1962. 1v. $20.

An excellent identification manual. Well illustrated. Index.

301 Burt, William Henry, and Grossenheider, R. P. Field guide to the mammals. 2d ed. rev. and enl. Houghton, 1964. 284p. $5.95.

Presents North American mammals and drawings, photographs, and brief notes on recognition, habitat, habits, young, range, and skulls. Subspecies have been omitted. Includes bibliography. Indexed.

302 Cochran, Doris M., and Goin, Coleman J. The new field book of reptiles and amphibians. Putnam, 1970. 359p. $5.95.

Concise and accurate descriptions in the most comprehensive field identification manual yet published. Because of its inadequate illustration, however, it should be supplemented by Roger Conant, *A Field Guide to Reptiles* (Houghton, 1958. 366p. $4.95).

303 Fisher, James, and others. Wildlife in danger. Viking, 1969. 368p. $12.95.

Arranged by zoological classifications: mammals, birds, reptiles, etc. Entries for each species in danger of extinction include description, status at the present time and measures being taken for protection and preservation. An important reference resource for the current concern with ecology and environment. Index.

304 International wildlife encyclopedia. Gen. eds., Maurice Burton and Robert Burton. Marshall Cavendish Corp. (distr. to schools and libraries by Purnell Library Service), 1969–70. 20v. $185.50.

Arranged in straight alphabetical order from aardvark in volume 1 through zovno in volume 20. Each volume is profusely illustrated, many illustrations in color. Content and style are suitable for use with elementary school children on up. Volume 20 contains topical indexes, by animals, by subjects, and by the zoological classification.

305 Miller, William C., and West, Geoffrey P. Encyclopedia of animal care. 9th ed. Williams and Wilkins, 1970. 1023p. $15.50.

Intended as a complete compendium of veterinary information for those responsible for the care or treatment of domesticated animals.

306 Moore, Clifford Bennett. Book of wild pets. C. T. Branford Co., 1954. 553p. $8.

Subtitle: "Being a discussion on the care and feeding of our native wildlife in captivity, together with notes on their identification and life habits." Bibliography.

307 Pennak, Robert William. Collegiate dictionary of zoology. Ronald, 1964. 583p. $9.50.

A useful dictionary containing about 19,000 definitions of zoological terms commonly not explained in zoological texts. Proper names are included.

308 Peterson, Roger Tory. Field guide to the birds: giving field marks of all species found east of the Rockies. 2d rev. and enl. ed. Houghton, 1947. 290p. $5.95, paper $2.95.

A well-illustrated guide to 702 forms of birds found east of the 100th meridian. Subspecies are listed only if field markings are obvious. Only the Eastern North American range is given for the birds covered. Libraries in the West will want *A Field Guide to Western Birds*. Libraries in border states will want both. Sponsored by the National Audubon Society.

309 ——— Field guide to western birds; field marks of all species found in North America west of the 100th meridian with a section on the birds of the Hawaiian Islands. 2d rev. and enl. ed. Houghton, 1961. 366p. $5.95.

Companion volume to Peterson's *A Field Guide to the Birds.* See no. 308.

310 Walker, Ernest Pillsbury. Mammals of the world. Johns Hopkins Univ. Pr., 1964, 3v. $45. v.1–2, 1500p. $30. v.3, Classified bibliography, 769p. $15.

The first systematic compendium of scientifically reliable information on mammals. Volumes 1 and 2 are arranged by orders, from "Manotremata" through "Pholidata." Volume 1 contains a "selected" bibliography covering the orders described in volumes 1 and 2. Indexes. Volume 3 is a thorough classified bibliography arranged by the orders of volumes 1 and 2. Designed for use as a separate unit or in conjunction with the first two volumes.

311 Whitney, Leon Fradley. Complete book of cat care. Doubleday, 1953. 284p. $5.95.

A systematic guide to cat care written by a veterinarian: grooming, feeding, diagnoses and ailments, and reproduction. Index.

Applied Sciences

Agriculture

312 U.S. Department of Agriculture. Yearbook of agriculture. Govt. Print. Off., 1936– . Annual. $3.80.

Each yearbook is devoted to a specific subject, e.g., *Farmer's World* (1964) and *Consumers All* (1965). Some of these, because of the subject, do not belong on the reference shelf, but others—such as those on *Trees* (1949), *Water* (1955), *Food* (1959), and *Seeds* (1961)—will be highly useful for a long time to come.

Electronics

313 Broadcasting yearbook. Broadcasting Publications, 1935– . Annual. Paper $13.50.

Contains 51 directories covering all phases of the broadcasting industry such as audience and market data, trade associations, technical and vocational schools. Index-tabbed categories.

314 Manly, Harold P. Drake's Radio-television electronics dictionary. Drake, 1971. unpaged. $5.95.

A dictionary of such terms as radio transmission and reception transisters, audio systems, and magnetism. Cross-reference within the text.

315 Hahn, Steven. Hi-fi handbook: a guide to monaural and stereophonic reproduction, 2d ed. rev. by William J. Kendall. Crowell, 1962. 216p. $5.95.

Highly practical reference work. A great deal of nontechnical information on understanding, evaluating, purchasing, and installing high-fidelity equipment. To update price and model information, reference should be made to *High Fidelity* or similar magazines.

316 Hicks, David E. Citizen's band radio handbook. 3d ed. Sams, 1968. 192p. $4.25.

The increasing number of people using the citizen's radio service makes this a highly useful book. Simple language, comprehensive, well illustrated.

317 Cooke, Nelson Magor, and Markus, John. Electronics and nucleonics dictionary. 3d ed. Ed. by John Markus. McGraw, 1966. 743p. $16.50.

Covers more than 16,000 terms used in fields ranging from radio and television to radar and nuclear science. Definitions presuppose no prior knowledge.

318 Radio amateur's handbook. American Radio, 1926– . Annual. $4.50.

The bible for "hams," this volume contains a wealth of information on equipment, operations, and regulations. It is also valuable for the amateur who wishes to obtain a license. Superseded editions should be put in the circulating collection.

319 Rogers, Harold A. Funk and Wagnalls dictionary of data processing terms. Funk and Wagnalls, 1970. 151p. $7.95.

Consists of those terms which have general applicability excluding those associated with particular processes, programs, or manufacturers. Acronyms, very important in this field, are entered with a cross-reference to the expanded form.

320 Stetka, Frank. NFPA handbook of the National electrical code. 2d ed. McGraw-Hill, 1969. 694p. $12.75.

"Based on the national electrical code, sponsored by the National fire protection association." Topics covered are wiring, design, methods, and materials; equipment; special occupancies and conditions; communication systems. For local regulations, copies of the municipal building code should also be available.

321 Television factbook. Television Digest, 1954– . Irregular. $25 (1968-69, no. 38)

Now in 2 volumes the first of which lists, describes and indicates radius of signal of television stations, arranged by state and city. Volume 2 is a directory of services to the television industry, arranged in classified order.

Engineering and Mechanics

322 Ralfe, Douglas. Airplanes of the world, 1490–1969. Rev. ed. Simon & Schuster, 1969. 440p. $7.50.

A historical survey of airplanes, military and civil, including a drawing and a description for each.

323 Brady, George S. Materials handbook: an encyclopedia for purchasing agents, engineers, executives, and foremen. 9th ed. McGraw-Hill, 1963. 968p. $19.50.

A long-established cyclopedic work of technical and trade information on approximately 12,000 materials of commercial importance, ranging from brick to walrus hide. Descriptive essays vary greatly in length; they include source, physical properties, and uses. Trade names are often mentioned. Includes a short but important section on economic geography.

324 Chilton's Foreign car repair manual. Chilton, 1971. 1497p. $14.50.

Covers German, Swedish, and Italian cars, arranged by country of manufacture and make.

325 Jones, Franklin Day, and Schubert, Paul B., eds. Engineering encyclopedia. 3d ed. Industrial Pr., 1963. 1431p. $15.

The best 1-volume work on engineering for the layman as well as for the practicing mechanic and technician.

326 Le Grand, Rupert, ed. New American machinist's handbook. Based on . . . American machinist's handbook. Ed. by Fred H. Colvin and

Frank A. Stanley. McGraw-Hill, 1955. Unpaged. $16.

A wealth of information on all aspects of metalworking. The 45 sections, separately paged, are each devoted to a specific aspect such as filing, grinding, fasteners, metal forming, or tool engineering.

327 Mason, Frances Kenneth, and Windrow, M. C., comps. Air facts and feats: a record of aerospace achievements. Doubleday, 1971. 223p. $8.95.

Similar in approach to the *Guinness Book of Records*. Lists under appropriate headings records and superlatives achieved in human flight.

328 Motor Service Magazine. Motor Service's automative encyclopedia. Ed. by William K. Toboldt and Larry Johnson. Goodheart-Wilcox, 1970. 768p. $9.96.

Libraries have a difficult time keeping the automotive books, yet they are essential reference tools. Both *Glenn* and this one are revised frequently and contain information on cars manufactured within the previous ten to fifteen years. Old editions, if they have not disappeared, should be kept. (Formerly *New Automotive Encyclopedia*.)

329 Motor's Auto repair manual. Hearst Magazines, Motor Book Division, 1938– . Annual. $10.95.

Mechanical repair procedures for American-made automobiles. Arranged by make of car. Index.

330 Peterson, Harold L., ed. Encyclopedia of firearms. Dutton, 1964. 367p. $14.95.

In dictionary format, entries cover all forms of small arms as well as biographical sketches for manufacturers and inventors. Bibliographies. Index.

Health and Medicine

331 Andrews, Mathew. Parent's guide to drugs. Doubleday, 1972. 186p. $6.95.

Describes the composition and effects of drugs such as LSD, the barbiturates and marijuana. Also includes a directory of organizations involved in drug education and sources of emergency aid. A list of films and a lexicon of drug slang.

332 Blakiston's New Gould medical dictionary. Ed. by Normand L. Hoerr and Arthur Osol. 2d ed. McGraw-Hill, 1956. 1463p. $13.50.

An authoritative dictionary of the terms in current use in all branches of medicine, allied health sciences as well as supporting theoretical disciplines such as botany and zoology. Illustrations. Tables.

333 Clark, Randolph Lee, and Cumley, Russell W., eds. Book of health. 2d ed. Van Nostrand, 1962. 888p. $17.50.

Clear, concise information for the layman on human diseases, the structure of the organs involved, and the healing treatment. 255 contributors. Highly readable. Well illustrated and indexed.

334 Cooley, Donald Gray, ed. Better Homes and Gardens family medical guide. Meredith Pr., 1964. 816p. $12.95.

Consists of twenty-five chapters, each by a specialist, which range over a broad terrain of general medical interest, e.g. infant and child care, laboratory tests, nutrition. Frequently, addresses of groups and organizations are given as sources of further information. Index.

335 Dorland's Illustrated medical dictionary. 24th ed. Saunders, 1965. 1724p. $13.50; deluxe ed. $17.

Frequently revised, this is the most widely used and most reliable of the medical dictionaries. Contains, along with definitions of current usage, lists of valuable information under such headings as "tests," "diseases," and "signs."

336 Drugs in current use and new drugs. Ed. by Walter Modell. Springer Publ., 1955– . Annual. Paper $3.25.

Pt. 1 is an alphabetical list of drugs currently used in clinical medicine. Entries give characteristics, properties, uses, modes of action, and precautions. Pt. 2 presents very detailed accounts of drugs new to the market. Useful to supplement *Merck* (no. 341) between editions.

337 New Encyclopedia of child care and guidance. Ed. by Sidonie Matsner Gruenberg. Doubleday, 1971. 1050p. $11.95.

In two parts: The first is an alphabetical arrangement by topic and will be of interest to parents and laymen in general. Contains a list of agencies and organizations and an annotated bibliography. The second part, "Basic Aspects of Child Development," is a series of articles by specialists which will be used by educators, psychologists, and counselors. Comprehensive, modern, and authoritative.

338 Gray, Henry. Anatomy of the human body. 28th ed. Lea & Febiger, 1966. 1448p. $25.

The classic text in the field and a standard reference tool. More than 1000 illustrations, nearly half in color, plus one of the most comprehensive and detailed indexes to be found in any reference book. Revised frequently.

339 Hammond (C. S.) and Company, Inc. Human anatomy atlas. Hammond, 1960. 36p. Paper $1.50.

32 full-color illustrations. Useful as an adjunct to *Gray* (no. 338).

340 Hinsie, Leland Earl, and Campbell, Robert Jean. Psychiatric dictionary. 4th ed. Oxford Univ. Pr., 1970. 816p. $19.50.

Somewhat advanced in level of definition but useful as a supplement to medical and general dictionaries. Includes psychosomatic medicine, adolescent and geriatric psychology, and drugs used in psychotherapy and psychoanalysis. Gives pronunciation, cites quotations showing use of term, and references.

341 Merck index: an encyclopedia of chemicals and drugs. 8th ed. Ed. by Paul G. Stecher. Merck, 1968. 1713p. $15.

Approximately 10,000 chemical substances are described, and properties such as boiling point, color, etc., are given. There are, in addition, some 42,000 proprietary and trade names cross-indexed. Medical and other uses are also provided.

342 Merck manual of diagnosis and therapy. 11th ed. Merck, 1966. 1850p. $7.50.

Provides physicians and informed laymen with the results of the latest research in the diagnosis and treatment of disease. Classified arrangement. Revised frequently. Index.

343 Physicians' desk reference to pharmaceutical specialities and biologicals. Medical Economics, 1947– . Annual. $9.

In five sections, lists and describes drugs and biologicals available from American manufacturers. Classified arrangement. Index.

344 Red Cross. U.S. American National Red Cross. First aid text book. 4th ed. rev. Doubleday, 1957. 241p. $1.50; paper $1.

Authoritative, concise, simply explained. Well illustrated. Latest edition only should be kept because of recent changes in artificial respiration, among other topics.

345 Sax, Newton Irving, and others, eds. Dangerous properties of industrial materials. 3d ed. Van Nostrand Reinhold, 1968. 1251p. $35.

Contains general information on toxicology, air pollution, radiation, etc. Main part of the work is an alphabetic arrangement of substances giving for each: general information, hazard analysis, countermeasures, cross-reference to general information section for storage and handling and for shipping regulations. A new section has been added on controlling environmental pollution.

House and Garden

346 Consumer bulletin. Consumers' Research, 1928– . Monthly. $5.

Contains reports of independent investigations of consumer products with recommendations on acceptability for purchase. Many special articles. Index.

347 Consumer reports. Consumer's Union, 1936– . Monthly. $6.

The approach is the same as that of *Consumer Bulletin* except that this journal covers a more diversified range of products. Index.

348 The Family Handyman Magazine's home emergencies and repairs. Harper, 1971. 212p. $6.95.

An intelligent approach to the amateur's attack on the malfunctions of domestic apparatus. Illustrated. Index.

349 Farmer, Fannie M. Fannie Farmer cook book. 11th rev. ed. by Wilma L. Perkins. Little, 1965. 624p. $6.95.

A classic that has served the American housewife for many years. Later editions have been thoroughly revised to include modern recipes and methods.

350 Funk and Wagnalls Dictionary Staff, eds. Cook's and diner's dictionary: a lexicon of food, wine, and culinary terms. Introduction by M. F. K. Fisher. Funk and Wagnalls, 1969. 274p. $6.95.

Reflecting its origin, this book's emphasis is on lexicography, e.g. etymologies, pronunciations, and extended definitions. Also contains biographies and is well illustrated. A useful supplement to standard cooking books.

351 Gladstone, Bernard. New York Times complete manual of home repair. Macmillan, 1966. 438p. $7.95.

Taken from the author's very popular column in the *New York Times,* this is an excellent collection of practical information on how to do it and how not to do it for the home handyman (and the not-so-handy). Illustrated.

352 Graf, Alfred Byrd. Exotic plant manual: fascinating plants to live with—their requirements, propa-

gation, and use. Roehrs (distr. by Scribner's), 1970. 839p. $27.50.

Contains a wealth of information on the origins, biology, physiology, and genetics of exotic or tropical plants. Instructions on their indoor care. Fully illustrated, many in color. Index.

353 Hardwick, Homer. Winemaking at home. Rev. ed. Funk & Wagnalls, 1970. 258p. $6.95.

A succinct guide to the preparation of those wines that most readily lend themselves to home manufacture. Index.

354 Kraus, Barbara. Calories and carbohydrates. Grosset & Dunlap, 1971. 322p. $7.95.

Lists 7500 brand names in alphabetical order giving carbohydrate and caloric content for each.

355 Montagné, Prosper. Larousse gastronomique: the encyclopedia of food, wine, and cookery. Ed. by Charlotte Turgeon and Nona Froud. Crown, 1961. 1101p. $20.

Recipes and food from all countries arranged in encyclopedic form. Illustrations, a few in color. Gastronomic maps of provinces of France. Index and bibliography in French. Text is in English.

356 Moore, Alma Chesnut. How to clean everything: an encyclopedia of what to use and how to use it. 3d ed. Simon & Schuster, 1968. 224p. $4.95; paper $1.95.

An excellent handbook to use in answering telephone reference questions.

357 New illustrated encyclopedia of gardening. Ed. by T. H. Everett. Greystone, 1960. 14v. $49.50.

Seeks to supply practical guidance to the cultivation of all those trees, shrubs, flowering plants, bulbs, fruits, and vege-

tables that are or may be grown in North America North of Mexico. Illustrated.

358 Rombauer, Irma von Starkloff, and Becker, Marion Rombauer. Joy of cooking. Rev. and enl. ed. Bobbs, 1967. 849p. $6.95.

A basic cookbook, somewhat more European in tone than *The Fannie Farmer Cook Book,* but excellent in the quality of its recipes and in its discussion of the preparation and serving of food.

359 Swezey, Kenneth M. Formulas, methods, and tips for home and workshop. Popular Science Publ., 1969. 691p. $7.95.

An eminently practical handbook, arranged by broad categories. Detailed index.

360 Watt, Bernice K., and Merrill, Annabel L. Composition of foods. Govt. Print. Off., 1963. 240p. Paper $1.50 (U.S. Dept. of Agriculture. Agricultural handbook, no. 8)

Primarily tables providing specifics on the nutrient values of foods.

361 The Wise encyclopedia of cookery: one of the world's most definitive reference books on food and cookery. Rev. and enl. Grosset & Dunlap, 1971. 1329p. $9.95.

Contains more than 5000 recipes and approximately 500 illustrations, charts, and diagrams. Index.

362 Wyman, Donald. Wyman's Gardening encyclopedia. Macmillan, 1971. 1222p. $17.50.

An excellent one-volume selective encyclopedia of gardening. Includes full botanical descriptions and nomenclatures of those plants treated. Selectivity consists in the author's exclusion of plants which he considers to be unacceptable for general cultivation. Dictionary arrangement with cross-references.

Copyright

363 Pilpel, Harriet F. Copyright guide, 4th ed. Bowker, 1969. 40p. $3.

A brief guide to copyright practice and law in question and answer format. Bibliography. Index.

Plastics and Textiles

364 Klapper, Marvin. Fabric almanac. 2d ed. Fairchild, 1971. 191p. $6.95.

A glossary of terms together with several factual sections on techniques, processes, and statistics.

365 Modern plastics encyclopedia. McGraw-Hill, 1941– . Annually in Sept. Available with a subscription to *Modern Plastics* (McGraw-Hill. Monthly. $12)

A directory of more than 4000 manufacturers of plastic materials and of machinery and equipment used in plastics manufacturing. Also includes related services to the industry and to individuals.

9 Art

Bibliographies and Indexes

366 Art index, 1929– : a cumulative author and subject index to a selected list of domestic and foreign periodicals and museum bulletins. Wilson. Quarterly (Jan., April, July, Oct.) with permanent, bound annual cumulations. Service basis.

Indexes 150 periodicals. Among the subject areas entered are archeology, architecture, fine arts, industrial design, photography, and films. A basic tool for libraries serving art conscious communities and subscribers to art periodicals. Volumes 1 through 17 (1929–69) are still available.

367 Carrick, Neville. How to find out about the arts: a guide to sources of information. Pergamon, 1965. 164p. $5.

Covers the fine arts in addition to photography and theatre. Includes facsimiles of specimen pages. Exercises at the end of chapters. Indexes.

368 Clapp, Jane. Art in Life. Scarecrow, 1959. 504p. $12.50. Supplement, 1965. 379p. $8.50.

The basic volume lists pictorial art reproductions which appeared in *Life* from 1936 through 1956 under artists, titles, and subjects. Also included are photographs of architecture, sculpture and the decorative arts. The *Supple-*

ment continues the indexing through 1963.

369 Ellis, Jessie Craft. Index to illustrations. Faxon, 1966. 682p. $12.50.

Indexes a highly selective list of widely owned books and periodicals such as *Current Biography* and *National Geographic*. Arranged by discrete subject.

370 Havlice, Patricia Pale. Art in Time. Scarecrow, 1970. 350p.

An index to all pictures which have been reproduced in the art section of *Time* from 1923 through 1969. Arranged by artists and painting. Birth and death dates of artists supplied, when possible, from other sources.

371 Vance, Lucille E., and Tracey, Esther M. Illustration index. 2d ed. Scarecrow. 1966. 527p. $12.

Revised and expanded subject index to 12 popular periodicals and a few books, 1950–June, 1963. Ready-reference source for photographs, charts, drawings, and paintings.

Dictionaries and Encyclopedias

372 Adeline, Jules. Adeline art dictionary, including terms in architecture, heraldry, and archeology. Trans. from the French. With a supplement of new terms by Hugo

G. Beigel. Ungar, 1966. 459p. $9.50.

Composed of ancient and modern terms, both technical and in general use. "A large amount of information has been incorporated from F. W. Fairholt's *Dictionary of Terms in Art*."

373 Cirker, Hayward, and Cirker, Blancher. Dictionary of American portraits: 4045 pictures of important Americans from earliest times to the beginning of the twentieth century. Dover, 1967. 756p. $30.

An alphabetically arranged archive of portraits of American men and women, not all U.S. nationals, who have made a significant contribution to our national life. Presidents and four other categories of prominent public persons have been continued beyond 1900. Portraits chosen are those which represent their subjects in the most characteristic poses. Reproductions are excellent. Bibliography and an occupational index to the subjects.

374 Encyclopedia of world art. McGraw-Hill, 1959–68. 15v. $597 the set; $50 a v.

An encyclopedic survey containing signed articles with extensive bibliographies. Covers architecture, sculpture, painting, and the minor arts. Numerous cross-references. Profusely illustrated. The definitive English-language encyclopedia. Volume 15 is a detailed index.

375 McGraw-Hill dictionary of art. Ed. by Bernard S. Meyers and Shirley D. Meyers. McGraw-Hill, 1969. 5v. $115.

An encyclopedic dictionary of the arts arranged by discrete topics from Aachen to the Zwinger Pavilion. Covers all periods, schools, and national traditions. Biographies. All articles are by specialists and longer ones are signed. Bibliographies. Numerous illustrations; some in color. No index but bountiful cross-references within the text. Not an abridgement of the *Encyclopedia of World Art* (no. 374) but an original work and one better suited to the needs of the smaller library.

376 Murray, Peter, and Murray, Linda. Dictionary of art and artists. Praeger, 1966 (c1959). 464p. $14.95.

Brief selected biographies chiefly of Western European artists, from about 1300 to the present day, and art terms not adequately defined in most general dictionaries. Illustrations make up the latter half of the volume. Useful for ready reference.

377 Oxford companion to art. Ed. by Harold Osborne. Oxford Univ. Pr., 1970. 1277p. $25.

A handbook of articles of varying lengths on the visual arts, not including handicrafts or the practical arts. Designed for the nonspecialist. Numerous cross-references. Most articles conclude with one or more coded references to the bibliography which numbers almost 3,000 items.

378 Praeger encyclopedia of art. Praeger, 1971. 5v. $150.

Contains approximately 4,000 entries arranged alphabetically. Based on, and in part translated from, a French work entitled *Dictionnaire universel de l'art et des artistes* (1967), this work reflects an advantageously different and complementing approach to its material from that taken by the *McGraw-Hill dictionary of art*. Both sets are needed.

379 Whittick, Arnold. Symbols, signs, and their meanings and their uses in design. 2d ed. Branford, 1971. 383p. $21.

Symbols in general, "traditional and familiar, their origins, meaning and history" in encyclopedic form. Includes bibliography for each symbol. Primarily intended to assist designers and artists who want to use symbols correctly. Well illustrated. Index.

Directories

380 American art directory, 1898– . Bowker. Triennial since 1952. $25.50.

Originally *American Art Annual*. Lists museums, art organizations, art departments in universities and colleges, art magazines, scholarships and fellowships, traveling exhibitions, and other miscellaneous information of interest to the art world. Mainly on United States, but does include Canada and a list of major museums and art schools abroad.

381 Museums directory of the United States and Canada. 2d ed. American Assn. of Museums and the Smithsonian Institution, 1965. 1039p. $7.50.

The standard directory for North America. Arranged by state (province) and then by city. Information includes address, officers, hours, major holdings, and activities. Covers museums in all fields: art, history, natural history, science, etc. Indexes.

History

382 Gardner, Helen. Art through the ages. Rev. by Horst de la Croix and Richard G. Tansey. 5th ed.

rev. and enl. Harcourt, 1970. 801p. $11.95.

Addressing the student and general reader, this history surveys Western art from early to modern times. The 5th edition, unlike earlier ones, excludes the arts of Asia and the Americas, and primitive art, concentrating instead on European art and its antecedents. Glossary, comprehensive index, bibliographies, other study aids, and an expanded program of illustrations.

383 Janson, Horst Woldemar, with Janson, Dora Jane. History of art: a survey of the major visual arts from the dawn of history to the present day. Rev. and enl. ed. Prentice-Hall and Abrams, 1969. 616p. $18.50.

Can be used as a textbook or as a scholarly reference source. The latest edition has expanded the section on "The Modern World" to emphasize developments in the past decade. Among the new features are end-paper maps showing all the sites mentioned in the text and a set of tables correlating the history of art with other important events in the history of man. Bibliography, index, and illustrations.

384 Spaeth, Eloise. American art museums: an introduction to looking. Rev. ed. McGraw-Hill, 1969. 321p. $8.95.

A statement of the characteristics and feeling of each museum and gallery and a description of the best or just selected pieces in each. The largest metropolitan museums are all grouped in one chapter, "The Big Seven." A limited number of college and university galleries are discussed. Arranged geographically. Illustrations.

Architecture

385 American architects directory. Ed.
by John F. Gane. 3d ed. Publ.
under the sponsorship of American Institute of Architects. Bowker, 1970. 1126p. $25.

Includes all members of the Institute,
except where omission has been re-
quested, and other eligible architects.
Omits most biographical facts not relevant to architectural training and practice. Arranged alphabetically with geographical index of architects.

386 Briggs, Martin Shaw. Everyman's
concise encyclopaedia of architecture. Dutton, 1960 (c1959). 372p.
$6.

Offers definitions, brief biographies, and
short articles on the history of architecture. References given for more important subjects. Line drawings and a
section of 32 plates.

387 Fletcher, *Sir* Banister Flight. History of architecture on the comparative method. 17th ed. rev. by
R. A. Cordingley. Scribner's, 1961.
1366p. $18.95.

The first major revision of a standard
reference work, profusely illustrated.
Features chapter bibliographies, a list
of general reference books, and a glossary of architectural terms.

388 Ramsey, Charles G., and Sleeper,
Harold R. Architectural graphic
standards. 6th ed. Wiley, 1970.
695p. $39.50.

Follows the 16-part uniform system
for the construction industry. Specifications and standards include tables, cal-
culations, and explanations. Bibliography. Index.

389 Ware, Dora, and Beatty, Betty.

Short dictionary of architecture,
including some common building
terms. With an introduction on
The study of architecture, by John
Gloag. [3d ed. rev. and enl.] Fern-
hill, 1961 (c1953). 136p. $3.

The standard dictionary in its field for
commonly-used terms in classical and
current architecture.

Sculpture

390 Clapp, Jane. Sculpture index.
Scarecrow, 1970. 2v. in 3. $65.
v.1, Europe and the contemporary
Middle East. 1146p. $30. v.2, pts.
1 and 2, The Americas, Orient,
Africa, Pacific, and Classical
world. 1369p. $35.

An artist, title, and selective subject
index to photographs of three-dimen-
sional sculptured art objects appearing
in anthologies, art histories, and museum catalogs. Also indexed are the
locations of the original works when
known. The long prefatory sections in
each volume contain lists of books indexed with identification symbols and
locations with their symbols. Introductory instructions for use are inade-
quately specified. Effective use requires
extensive examination in order to sort
out all of the work's numerous data
elements which include, in addition to
those mentioned, artists with their
dates and nationalities, dimensions of
the sculptured piece, material in which
rendered, variant and translated titles,
e.g. "Le Penseur"—"The Thinker," etc.

391 The new dictionary of modern
sculpture. Gen. ed., Robert Maillard. Tudor, 1971. 328p.

Presented as a "fervent apology" for
twentieth-century sculpture. Signed entries contain a brief biography, some

technical information and criticism. Arranged alphabetically by sculptor.

Ceramics

392 Chaffers, William. Marks and monograms on European and Oriental pottery and porcelain. The British section ed. by Geoffrey A. Godden. The European and Oriental sections ed. by Frederick Litchfield and R. L. Hobson. 15th rev. ed. Borden, 1965. 2v. $19.95.
Usually considered the standard work on pottery marks. Bibliography.

393 Cushion, J. P., and Honey, William Bowyer. Handbook of pottery and porcelain marks. 3d ed. Faber, 1965. 476p. $7.65.
Includes many nineteenth- and twentieth-century marks, as well as earlier ones. Arranged by country; includes Europe, China, and Japan. Good index.

394 Eberlein, Harold Donaldson, and Ramsdell, Roger Wearne. Practical book of chinaware. Rev. ed. Lippincott, 1948. 320p. $10.
Answers questions on the less-rare types of china which are likely to be considered treasures by average collectors. Covers the china of all countries. Bibliography; 120 plates, a few in color.

Art Metalwork

395 Wyler, Seymour B. Book of old silver, English, American, foreign. With all available hallmarks, including Sheffield plate marks. Crown, 1937. 447p. $6.95.
A comprehensive, indexed table of hallmarks facilitates identification of silver. Contains chapters on various types of silver articles, e.g., tea and condiment sets, flat and table ware, boxes, etc.

Decorative Arts and Design

396 Aronson, Joseph. New encyclopedia of furniture. Deluxe ed. Crown, 1967. 484p. $15.
Easy access to brief information, illustrated with photographs and line cuts. Glossary of designers and craftsmen; bibliography. Special section on the use of color.

397 Bernasconi, John R. Collectors' glossary of antiques and fine arts. Transatlantic Arts, 1966. 587p. $11.50.
Of interest to the collector and to those in the antiques business, also to libraries because of the amount of useful information. An excellent source, also, for symbols in classical, religious, heraldic, and Chinese arts.

398 Boger, Louise Ade. The complete guide to furniture styles. Enl. ed. Scribner's, 1969. 500p. $17.50.
With the exception of a final chapter on Chinese styles, the work is confined to the European and American traditions. Arrangement is chronological. Profusely illustrated. Bibliography. Index of artists and craftsmen.

399 Boger, Louise Ade, and Boger, H. Batterson. Dictionary of antiques and the decorative arts: a book of reference for glass, furniture, ceramics, silver, periods, styles, technical terms, etc. 2d ed. Scribner's, 1967. 662p. $17.50.
Alphabetically arranged entries cover America, Europe, and the Orient. Brief biographies and brief period histories. Revised edition contains supplement de-

fining 700 new terms and brief biographies.

400 Comstock, Helen, ed. Concise encyclopedia of American antiques, Hawthorn, 1965. 848p. $14.95.
Originally issued in two volumes in 1958. Does not contain material reprinted from the *Connoisseur's Concise Encyclopedia of Antiques,* 1955–61 (now out of print), but is a comprehensive work of new material written by authorities in their various fields. Treats some obscure pieces, hard to find in antique books: marine prints, folk art, firearms, theater and circus playbills, etc. Bibliographies.

401 Coysh, A. W. The antique buyer's dictionary of names. Praeger, 1970. 278p. $12.50.
Arranged in 17 sections, e.g. book illustration, chinaware, furniture. Provides information on artists, designers, firms, and craftsmen. Appended to each section is a list of further readings. Its chief value is its reliability as an identification guide.

402 Hayward, Helena, ed. Connoisseur's handbook of antique collecting: a dictionary of furniture, silver, ceramics, glass, fine art, etc. Hawthorn, 1960. 320p. $5.95.
A useful work, perhaps most valuable for definition of terms. Includes historical outlines and a select bibliography.

403 Kamm, Minnie Elizabeth (Watson). Encyclopedia of antique pattern glass. Serry Wood, pseud., ed. Century House, 1961. 2v. $25.
Describes collectable standard pattern glass from the nineteenth century to about 1915. Arranged by names of patterns.

404 Macdonald-Taylor, Margaret Stephens. Dictionary of marks, metalwork, furniture, ceramics: the identification handbook for antique collectors. Hawthorn, 1962. 318p. $5.95.
A guide to the identification of American, English, and Continental antiques. Section on ceramics lists Japanese date marks and Chinese reign marks. Bibliography.

405 McKearin, George Skinner, and McKearin, Helen. American glass. 2,000 photos, 1,000 drawings by James L. McCreery. Crown, 1948. 850p. $14.95.
History of the development of glassmaking in America and guide for the identification of American glass.

406 Meyer, Franz Sales. Handbook of ornament: a grammar of art, industrial and architectural designing in all its branches for practical as well as theoretical use. Dover, 1957. 548p. Paper $2.95.
A republication of a standard handbook. Well illustrated and indexed.

407 Miller, Edgar George. American antique furniture, a book for amateurs. Dover, 1966. 2v. Paper $10.
Entries and illustrations, arranged by type. Shows changes of style in successive periods. Stresses important features for those who wish to live with antiques. Volume 2 lists museums and collections in New England open to the public.

408 Pegler, Martin. Dictionary of interior design. Crown, 1966. 500p. $7.50.
Concise definitions covering elements

of interior design, old and new, from horsehair to furniture. Small illustrations with text. Includes brief biographies about individuals in design and associated fields.

409 Savage, George. Dictionary of antiques. Praeger, 1970. 534p. $17.50.
Designed for collectors and dealers who need to date or attribute antiques of all kinds, including plate, glassware, furniture, embroidery, etc. Numerous cross-references. Illustrations, many in color. Bibliography.

410 Shull, Thelma. Victorian antiques. Tuttle, 1963. 421p. $12.75.
A guide to the objects of art, utilitarian or otherwise, made during the Victorian period and to their use, such as "language of the fan." Bibliography and illustrations.

411 Speltz, Alexander. Styles of ornament. 2d ed. Dover, 1960. 647p. Paper $3.
Aims to represent "the entire range of ornament in all its different styles from pre-historic times 'till the middle of the 19th century." A republication of David O'Conor's translation from the second German edition. Bibliography.

Painting

412 Bartran, Margaret. A guide to color reproductions. 2d ed. Scarecrow, 1971. 625p. $15.
Lists art reproductions in sheet form available in the United States from commercial print dealers. Arranged in serially numbered order by artist giving size of print, name of dealer, and price. Index by title.

413 Encyclopedia of painting: painters and painting of the world from prehistoric times to the present day. Bernard S. Myers, ed. 3d rev. ed. Crown, 1970. 576p. $14.95.
Definitions of technical terms, histories of movements in painting, lengthy articles on painting in various countries, and biographies of great painters are arranged in dictionary form. Illustrations, many in color, accompany text. The third edition adds 200 articles and 150 illustrations.

414 Haftmann, Werner. Painting in the twentieth century. Rev. ed. Praeger, 1965. 2v. $17.50; paper $3.95. Picture ed. (v.2), paper $5.95.
A definitive survey and comprehensive analysis of twentieth-century painting. Biographical section contains more than 400 listings.

415 Dictionary of modern painting. Ed. by Carlton Lake and Robert Maillard. Tudor, 1960. 310p. $8.95.
A biographical and critical dictionary of modern painters, the Impressionists up to artists of the present day. Contributions are signed and of varying lengths. Well illustrated.

416 Mayer, Ralph. Artist's handbook of material and techniques. 3d rev. ed. Viking, 1970. 750p. $10.
Excellent guide for the amateur and professional. With this in the reference collection, both Doerner, *Materials of the Artist,* and Taubes, *Guide to Traditional and Modern Painting Methods,* can be put into the circulating collection.

417 Monro, Isabel S., and Monro, Kate M. Index to reproductions of

American paintings, and first supplement. Wilson, 1948, 1964. 731p., 480p. $12.50; $15.

An index to reproductions in 520 books and more than 300 exhibition catalogs by name of artist, title of painting, and subject. Locations of the original paintings are given when known.

418 ———— Index to reproductions of European paintings. Wilson, 1956. 668p. $12.50.

A guide to pictures by European artists that are reproduced in 328 books. Paintings are entered under name of artist, title of painting, and, in many cases, subject. Locations of original paintings are noted whenever known.

419 New York Graphic Society. Fine art reproductions of old and modern masters: a comprehensive illustrated catalog of art through the ages. 8th rev. ed. The Society, 1968. 420p. $25.

Primarily intended as a catalog of prints distributed by the New York Graphic Society, this volume offers an extensive pictorial history of painting through the ages. Dates of artists and of painting, location of originals, and size and price of prints are noted under each illustration.

420 United Nations Educational, Scientific and Cultural Organization. Catalogue of colour reproductions of paintings prior to 1860. 8th ed. rev. and enl. UNESCO (distr. by International Publications Service), 1968. 451p. Paper $8.50.

421 ———— Catalogue of reproductions of paintings, 1860–1969. 9th ed. UNESCO (distr. by International Publications Service), 1969. 549p. Paper $8.50.

Small black-and-white reproductions, together with size, price, and publisher, provide the information necessary for purchasing color reproductions available from various publishers.

Photography

422 Encyclopedia of photography: the complete photographer: the comprehensive guide and reference for all photographers. Willard D. Morgan, general ed. Greystone (distr. by Hawthorn), 1967. 20v. $3.98 each.

Designed to meet the needs of photographers at all levels of technical proficiency. Treats all phases of the art: procedures, techniques, and equipment. Arranged alphabetically by specific subject. Each volume has a separate table of contents with a combined contents summary in volume 1. Bibliography and indexes in volume 20.

423 The Focal encyclopedia of photography. Focal Pr. (distr. by Pitman), 1966. 2v. $39.

Contains 2,400 articles contributed by 281 specialists. A tripartite arrangement: dictionary of terms, encyclopedia of aesthetic theory and technical history, and a practical guide to photographic practice. Illustrated. Cross-reference within text. Bibliographic references appended to major articles.

424 Manual of photography: formerly the Ilford manual of photography. Ed. by Alan Horder. 6th ed. Chilton, 1971. 596p. $15.95.

An up-to-date, reliable version of a classic which has been published at intervals since 1891. Fully current with the most recent technical, aesthetic, and industrial developments.

Costume

425 Davenport, Millia. Book of costume. Crown, 1964. 480p. $12.95. (Reprint of 1948 ed.)
Originally in two volumes, but now available in this one-volume edition. Basic information ends in 1867. Includes costumes of the Orient, Europe, and America, as well as ecclesiastical vestments, habits of monastic orders, and the dress of the Roman army. Arranged chronologically. Many excellent illustrations, with location of original for a majority. Detailed index.

426 Evans, Mary. Costume through the ages. 3d ed. Lippincott, 1950. 360p. $8.95.
An excellent introduction to the subject. Many illustrations. Bibliographies for each chapter and a general bibliography. Index.

427 Payne, Blanche. History of costume: from the ancient Egyptians to the twentieth century. Harper, 1965. 607p. $13.95.
Fully illustrated with photographs of paintings, statuary, and actual costumes, as well as with line drawings. Accessories and 50 pages of draft patterns are featured. Concluding date is 1900. Bibliography; detailed index.

428 Wilcox, Ruth Turner. Dictionary of costume. Scribner's, 1969. 406p. $15.
A fully illustrated dictionary of historic costume in all of its facets on a worldwide basis. Entries provide succinct descriptions of the item of clothing. Bibliography.

429 ——— Five centuries of American costume. Scribner's, 1963. 207p. $10.
The dress of American men, women, and children, from the Vikings, Eskimos, and early settlers to 1960. Arranged chronologically. Clear line drawings illustrate the text. Bibliography. Lacks an index.

10 Music

Bibliographies and Indexes

430 Charms, Désirée de, and Breed, Paul F. Songs in collections: an index. Information Service, 1966. 588p. O.P.

Analyzes 411 collections for more than 9,000 songs, folk songs, carols, and sea chanties. A much needed supplement to the older Sears' *Song Index*.

431 Music index: the key to current music periodical literature. Information Service, 1949– . Monthly (cumulates annually). $275 a yr.

Indexes approximately 270 current periodicals under authors and subjects. Contains book review citations. Annual cumulations are slow to appear necessitating reference to monthly issues—for several years.

432 Sears, Minnie E., ed., assisted by Phyllis Crawford. Song index: an index to more than 12,000 songs. 648p. 1926. Song index supplement: an index to more than 7,000 songs. 366p. 1934. Shoe String, 1966. 2v. in 1. $27.50. (Reprint of earlier Wilson eds.)

Lists titles, first lines, authors' names, and composers' names in a single alphabet with fullest information under title entry. Can be used to find words and music of a song, lists of songs by

an author or composer, and poems which have been set to music.

433 Shapiro, Nat. Popular music: an annotated index of American popular songs. Adrian. v.1, 1950–59 (1964); v.2, 1940–49 (1965); v.3, 1960–64 (1966); v.4, 1930–39 (1968); v.5, 1920–29 (1969). $16 each.

A selected list of popular songs published 1920–64 arranged by year, then alphabetically by title; gives author, title, composer, publisher, and first or best selling record, indicating performer and record company. Each volume has a title index and a directory of music publishers.

Dictionaries and Encyclopedias

434 Apel, Willi. Harvard dictionary of music. 2d ed. Rev. and enl. Harvard Univ. Pr., 1969. 935p. $20.

Restricted to musical topics such as forms, techniques, and instruments. Excludes biographies. Designed to meet the needs of amateurs, professionals, and musical scholars. Bibliographies. Some of the longer articles are signed. Based on the 1st (1944) edition, Willi Apel, and Ralph T. Daniel's *Harvard Brief Dictionary of Music* (Washington Square Pr., 1960. 341p. paper $1.25) is more limited in scope in that it is directed primarily to the amateur, excluding the more scholarly information present in the parent volume.

435 Cross, Milton, and Ewen, David. The Milton Cross new encyclopedia of great composers and their music. Doubleday, 1969. 2v. $11.95.
Directed to the comparatively uninformed layman. In addition to biographies of musicians includes sections on the orchestra, the history of music, and a dictionary of musical terms. Index.

436 Ewen, David. New encyclopedia of the opera. Rev. ed. Hill & Wang, 1971. 759p. $15.
Comprehensive source book on opera, including opera plots, history, characters in operas, premieres, biographies of performers, etc. Includes a separate pronunciation guide.

437 Feather, Leonard G. Encyclopedia of jazz. New ed. Horizon, 1960. 527p. $15.

438 —— Encyclopedia of jazz in the sixties. Horizon, 1967. 312p. $15; boxed with Encyclopedia of jazz as a set $25.
Articles and polls on jazz, lists of jazz recordings, and brief biographies of all important jazz musicians. Includes calendar of musicians' birthdays, birthplaces of musicians by state and town, a list of jazz organizations, schools and booking agencies, jazz record companies.

439 Grove, *Sir* George. Grove's Dictionary of music and musicians. Ed. by Eric Blom. 5th rev. ed. enl., 1954. Supplementary v. (v.10) to 5th ed. by Eric Blom and Enis

Stevens. St. Martin's, 1961. 10v. $149.50; $15 a v.
Covers thoroughly all aspects of music, composers, and performers.

440 Roxon, Lillian. Rock encyclopedia. Grosset & Dunlap, 1969. 611p. $9.95.
Devoted to career information and the discography of rock groups and individual performers. Some attention given to the vocabulary of rock argot.

441 Salem, James M. A guide to critical reviews. pt. 2: The musical from Rodgers and Hart to Lerner and Lowe. Scarecrow, 1967. 353p. $9.
Arranged alphabetically by title and by season: 1920–21 through 1965–66. Review citations are from general American and Canadian periodicals and the *New York Times*. Information on long runs, awards and prizes. Indexes by authors, composers, lyricists; directors, designers, choreographers; by original works and authors; and by titles.

442 Stambler, Irwin. Encyclopedia of popular music. St. Martin's, 1965. 359p. $10.
A selective compendium of materials covering composers, songs, performers, and terminology of popular music. Also a section on awards.

443 Thompson, Oscar, ed. International cyclopedia of music and musicians. Ed. by Robert Sabin. 9th ed. rev. and enl. Dodd, 1964. 2476p. $35.
Considering the size and price, this is the best 1-volume work in the field. Appendix gives pronunciation of names and titles.

Guides and Handbooks

444 Ewen, David, ed. American popu-
lar songs from the Revolutionary
War to the present. Random
House, 1966. 507p. $10.
Approximately 3,600 songs sung by
Americans throughout their history.
Cites for each the date, composer, lyri-
cist, and films or Broadway musicals
in which they have been featured.
American composers listed in an ap-
pendix.

445 ——— New complete book of
the American musical theatre.
Holt, 1970. 800p. $15.
Primarily useful for its chronology of
shows from 1866 to 1970. Biographical
data on composers, lyricists, and libret-
tists over the same time span. Index.

446 Fuld, James J. Book of world-
famous music: classical, folk, and
popular. Rev. ed. Crown, 1971.
566p. $12.50.
No other title really quite does what
this book does. Several thousand songs,
tunes, etc., are alphabetically indexed
with the musical theme, and words,
where applicable, are printed along
with a brief history of the melody.
Also gives brief biographical data on
composers and lyricists.

447 Haywood, Charles, ed. Folk songs
of the world. Day, 1966. 320p.
$10.95.
Contains the words (in original language and English translation) and
music of 180 songs from 119 countries,
with historical background and notes
on each song. Discusses musical culture
of each area. Bibliography; selected
list of recordings; and index of first
lines.

448 Kinsley, James, ed. Oxford book
of ballads. Oxford Univ. Pr.,
1969. 816p. $8.50.
Completely revised from the 1910 edition. Includes close to eighty English
and Scottish ballads, street ballads, and
broadsides.

449 Kobbé, Gustav. Kobbé's Complete
opera book. Rev. ed. by *Lord
Harewood*. Putnam, 1963. 1262p.
$10.95.
Detailed description of each of the important operas with musical quotations,
plot synopses, characters, historical
background, etc. Arranged by centuries and subdivided into countries. Illustrated and indexed.

450 Lawless, Ray McKinley. Folksing-
ers and folksongs in America. 2d
ed. Duell (distr. by Hawthorn),
1965. 750p. $10.
Detailed handbook of American folk
music, including biographies, bibliographies, discography, information about
folklore societies and folk festivals, etc.
Reprint of 1960 edition with a supplement that updates earlier information.

451 Mattfeld, Julius. Variety music
cavalcade, 1620–1969: a chronology of vocal and instrumental
music popular in the United States.
3d. ed. Prentice-Hall, 1971. 766p.
$15.
A record of songs achieving popularity
in each year from 1620 to 1969 within
the cultural setting which is also succinctly summarized for each year. Index of song titles.

452 Nettl, Paul. National anthems. 2d
enl. ed. Trans. by Alexander Gode.
Ungar, 1967. 261p. $5.50.
Arranged geographically, this edition

covers 114 countries and provides complete history for each anthem. Music is not given. Index.

453 Scholes, Percy A. Oxford companion to music. Ed. by J. O. Ward. 10th ed. Oxford Univ. Pr., 1970. 1189p. $25.

A standard dictionary covering all areas of musical interest. Some articles are encyclopedic, others are quite short.

Numerous cross-references from specific entries to more comprehensive ones.

454 Slonimsky, Nicolas. Music since 1900. 4th ed. Scribner's, 1971. 1595p. $49.50.

Contains a descriptive chronology, brief biographies, a glossary of musical terms and selected documents of 20th century music. Index.

11 Cinema, Dance, and Theater

Cinema

455 Dimmitt, Richard Bertrand. An actor's guide to the talkies: a comprehensive listing of 8000 feature-length films from January, 1949 until December, 1964. Scarecrow, 1967–68. 2v. $35.

Volume 1 lists 8000 feature-length films with production dates and supplying full information on casts. Volume 2 is an index by actors' names.

456 ———— A title guide to the talkies. Scarecrow, 1965. 2v. $47.50.

Lists 16,000 feature-length motion pictures from October, 1927, until December, 1963, in alphabetical order. Gives title, company producing, date of release, and source from which adapted. A valuable source of information in connection with reruns on television.

457 Enser, A. G. S. Filmed books and plays: a list of books and plays from which films have been made, 1928–1967, with a supplementary list for 1968 and 1969. Rev. ed. Andre Deutsch, 1971. 509p. 84 shillings.

An excellent working list, not claimed to be exhaustive, of British and American films made from books and plays.

Arranged in three sections: film titles, authors, and changes of original titles. Same sequence repeated for the supplementary list.

458 Halliwell, Leslie. Filmgoer's companion. With a foreword by Alfred Hitchcock. 3d ed. rev. and enl. Hill & Wang, 1970. 1917p. $15.

A dictionary with brief entries for directors, cinematographers, composers, actors, films, cinematic themes, and related subjects, some being essay length. Emphasizes the British and American film scene since 1930, although the films of Europe are not neglected.

459 International motion picture almanac. Ed. by Richard Gertner. Quigley, 1929– . Annual. $13.

Useful for quickly finding out when a motion picture was released. Lists producers, exhibitors, motion-picture companies, and other essential data of the motion-picture world.

460 International television almanac. Ed. by Richard Gertner and associates. Quigley, 1956– . Annual. $13.

Does essentially for television what the *International Motion Picture Almanac* does for motion pictures.

461 Limbacher, James L. Feature films on 8mm and 16mm: a directory of feature films available for rental, sale and lease in the United States. 3d ed. Bowker, 1971. 300p. $13.50.
Films are listed alphabetically by title. Index of directors. Prices are not included.

462 Michael, Paul, and others, eds. The American movie reference book: the sound era. Prentice-Hall, 1969. 629p. $29.95.
Provides dates and full credits for 1,000 popular American films. A brief history of the U.S. cinema and a who's who of actors. Bibliography. Index.

463 ———, and Parish, James Robert. The Emmy awards: a pictorial history. Crown, 1970. 384p. $9.95.
Complete coverage of the Emmy awards for 1948 through 1968, with addendum for 1969–70. Year-by-year breakdown.

464 Salem, James M. A guide to critical reviews. pt. 4: The screenplay from The Jazz Singer to Dr. Strangelove. Scarecrow, 1971. 2 v. 1420p. $30. v.1, A–J; v.2, K–Z.
A title listing of approximately 12,000 American and foreign screenplays derived from Dimmitt's *A Title Guide to the Talkies* to which the reader is referred for bibliographic and production data on the films listed. Review citations from general American and Canadian periodicals and the *New York Times.* Supplementary information on the Academy Awards. No indexes.

465 Shipman, David. The great movie stars: the golden years. Crown, 1970. 576p. $10.

Lists 181 stars reaching prominence before the end of World War II. The arrangement is alphabetical. The style and approach are unconventionally irreverent. Illustrated. Index.

466 Weaver, John T. Twenty years of silents, 1908–1928. Scarecrow, 1971. 514p.
In three parts, alphabetically by players and by directors and producers, and geographically by film studios.

467 Spigelgass, Leonard, ed. Who wrote the movie and what else did he write?: an index to screen writers and their film works, 1936–1969. Academy of Motion Picture Arts and Sciences/Writers Guild of America, 1969. 491p. $45.
This generously revealing title tells the full story of the book. Ably corrects an imbalance in the general public consciousness: movies have script writers as well as actors and directors. Film title index.

Dance

468 Balanchine, George. Balanchine's New complete stories of the great ballets. Ed. by Francis Mason. Drawings by Marta Becket. Rev. and enl. ed. Doubleday, 1968. 626p. $10.
Detailed stories of more than 200 standard ballets, both classic and modern, presently or likely to be in the repertoires of the world's companies. Balanchine discusses history, appreciation, children's ballets, careers in ballet, dancers, and choreography, among other subjects. Features an illustrated glossary, bibliography, and an annotated guide to ballet recordings.

469 Chujoy, Anatole, and Manchester, P. W., comps. The dance encyclopedia. Rev. and enl. ed. Simon & Schuster, 1967. 992p. $20.

Encyclopedic articles on the many forms of the dance combined with short entries on persons and technical terms. Signed articles. Illustrations.

Theater

470 Chicorel, Marietta, ed. Chicorel theater index to plays in anthologies, periodicals, discs and tapes. Chicorel Library Publ. Co., 1970– . v.1, 573p. $23.50 (1970), v.2, 502p. $37.50 (1971).

The first two volumes index plays appearing in anthologies and periodicals. In each there is a main section comprising entries under author, play, title, anthology title and editor's name. Full bibliographic information provided including price if the item is in print. Indexes by author, play, editor, and by subject indicators.

471 Ottemiller, John Miller. Ottemiller's Index to plays in collections: an author and title index to plays appearing in collections published between 1900 and mid-1970. Ed. by John M. Connor and Billie M. Connor, 5th ed. rev. & enl. Scarecrow, 1971. 452p. $11.

Indexes 3049 plays appearing in 1047 collections published in the United States and Great Britain. Arrangement is alphabetical by author, listing plays and coded references to anthologies. Title index.

472 Anderson, Michael, ed. Crowell's Handbook of contemporary drama. Crowell, 1971. 505p. $10.

Concentrates on drama as literature, not as theater, in Europe and the Americas since World War II. Includes surveys of drama by country, biographies and critical assessments of playwrights, evaluation of representative plays and discussions of theatrical influences that have affected the development of contemporary dramatic form.

473 Drury, Francis Keese Wynkoop. Drury's Guide to best plays. 2d ed. Ed. by James M. Salem. Scarecrow, 1969. 512p. $15.

As was Drury's own edition, this is arranged alphabetically by playwright. Brief synopses, cast analyses, sources in which available (anthologies and play reprint publishers, e.g. French) and royalty charges for amateur productions. Indexes: by cast; co-authors, original authors; titles.

474 Freedley, George, and Reeves, John A. History of the theatre. 3d. rev. ed. Crown, 1968. 1024p. $10.

Comprehensive world history of the theater from its beginnings in ancient Egypt to 1940, with supplement for period 1940–66, covering in chronological fashion the gradual evolution of drama as set against a background of political, religious, and social phenomena. Annotated bibliographies for main part of work and supplement. Illustrated.

475 Gassner, John, and Quinn, Edward, eds. The reader's encyclopedia of world drama. Crowell, 1969. 1030p. $15.

A succinct world-wide consideration of drama as literature and not as theater. Plot résumés of many plays. Discussions of dramatic trends. No index.

476 Hartnoll, Phyllis, ed. Oxford companion to the theatre. 3d ed. Oxford Univ. Pr., 1967. 1088p. $15.
One-volume encyclopedia, covering all aspects of the theater in all countries and all periods up to the end of 1964, and to later dates for England, France, and the United States. Bibliography and illustrations.

477 Keller, Dean H. Index to plays in periodicals. Scarecrow, 1971. 558p. $15.
An index to plays appearing in 103 selected periodicals. Arranged by playwright and play. Title index. Supplements other play indexes.

478 Play index, 1949–1952, 1953–1960, 1961–1967. Wilson, 1953–68. 3v. $35.
Each volume is arranged as follows: a main list by author, title, and subject; collections indexed and an analysis by cast composition.

479 Salem, James M. A guide to critical reviews. pt. 1: American drama from O'Neill to Albee. Scarecrow, 1966. 181p. $4.50.
Arranged by author and play. Reviews cited are those which have appeared in general American and Canadian periodicals and the *New York Times*. Scholarly journals are excluded. Title index.

480 ———— A guide to critical reviews. pt. 2: British and continental drama from Ibsen to Pinter. Scarecrow, 1968. 309p. $7.
Covers plays from 1909 to 1966. Arranged by playwright and play. Cites reviews in general American and Canadian periodicals and the *New York Times*. Miscellaneous information on dramatists, productions, and awards. Indexes by authors, adaptors, and translators, and by titles.

481 Simon's Directory of theatrical materials, services and information. Package Publicity Service, 1955– . Irregular $5.
A classified directory ranging from actor's agents to wigs.

12 Games, Sports, and Hobbies

Games

482 Foster, Robert F. Foster's Complete Hoyle. Rev. ed. Lippincott, 1963. 697p. $5.95.
Subtitle: "An encyclopedia of games, including all indoor games played today, with suggestions for good play, illustrative hands and all official laws to date, revised and enlarged with complete laws of contract bridge and canasta."

483 Sunnucks, Anne, comp. The encyclopedia of chess. St. Martin's, 1970. 587p. $10.
An encyclopedic treatment of chess including all technical, biographic, statistical, and directory facets of the game. All entries appear in dictionary order including those which list winners of championships. Index.

Sports

484 The baseball encyclopedia: the complete and official record of major league baseball. Macmillan, 1970. 2337p. $25.
A complete statistical record. A season-by-season presentation. Introductory material on the history of the game. An appendix listing sources of information.

485 Chester, David. Olympic games handbook. Scribner's, 1971. 277p. $7.95; paper $2.45.
Begins with 1896 and concludes with the Winter Olympiad of 1968. Indicates who won what events; times, distances, records, etc.; and the existing records at any given point in time. Illustrated. No index.

486 Golf magazine's encyclopedia of golf. Ed. by Robert Schoof. Harper & Row, 1970. 424p. $13.95.
The full spectrum of statistical, biographical, historical, and directory information of interest to all devotees. Topical arrangement. No index.

487 Hollander, Zander, ed. The modern encyclopedia of basketball. Four Winds, 1969. 468p. $12.95.
Complete coverage of basketball; its history, teams, individual stars, records, and rules. Bibliography. Index.

488 Menke, Frank Grant. Encyclopedia of sports. Revisions ed. by Roger Treat. 4th rev. ed. Barnes, 1969. 1100p. $20.
Comprehensive historical, statistical, legendary, and instructional details of nearly 80 sports. Winners and their records are given for each sport in chronological order.

489 Ormond, Clyde. Outdoorsman's handbook. Outdoor Life & Dutton, 1970. 336p. $5.95.

A recreation and survival manual for the hiker, camper, fisherman, and hunter. Excellent practical advice on crisis-dictated improvisations. Index.

490 Sports rules encyclopedia: the official rules for 38 sports and games. National Pr., 1961. 563p. $11.90.

Contains official rules, with diagrams and charts, of 38 games and sports that can be played at the high school and college level. Gives name and address of organization furnishing rules for each sport.

491 Treat, Roger. Official encyclopedia of football. 9th rev. ed. Barnes, 1971. 655p. $12.

Includes data on players and coaches of collegiate and professional football teams from the sport's inception to the present day. Rules, scoring, and records. The definitive work on this subject needed when *Menke* (no. 488) proves insufficient.

Hobbies

492 Andrews, Charles J. Fell's United States coin book. 7th rev. ed. Fell, 1970. 156p. $3.95.

Covers the coinages of the United States. Gives current values of issues. Notes on evaluation, selling, and collecting. Index.

493 Di Valentin, Maria, and others. Practical encyclopedia of crafts. Drawings by Louis Di Valentin and others. Sterling, 1970. 544p. $20.

Arranged under ten main headings such as clay, paper, wood. Articles on crafts stress techniques and materials. Illustrated. Bibliography.

494 Graumont, Paoul, and Hensel, John. Encyclopedia of knots and fancy rope work. 4th ed. compl. rev. & enl. Cornell Maritime Pr., 1958. 690p. $15.

A survey of the rope splicing and knotting lore, nautical, land based, and recreational. Descriptions and instructions are provided for all known knots. Glossary. Index.

495 Guide book of United States coins. Ed. by R. S. Yeoman. Whitman, 1946– . Annual. $2.50.

Catalog and price list of coins from A.D. 1616 to date, including early tokens, commemorative issues, proofs, etc., as well as a brief history of American coinage. Illustrated.

496 Hobson, Burton, and Obojski, Robert. Illustrated encyclopedia of world coins. Doubleday, 1970. 512p. $12.95.

An excellent introductory identification handbook for novice collectors. Covers coinages of the ancient, medieval, and modern worlds. Index.

497 Lovell, Eleanor Cook, and Hall, Ruth Mason. Index to handicrafts, model-making and workshop. Faxon, 1936. 476p. $9.

Supplements 1–4 (1943–69), $9, $10, $14, and $10, respectively. Supplement 3 is by Amy Winslow and Harriet Turner. Supplement 4 is by E. Winifred Alt. The basic volume plus four supplements are, respectively, nos. 57, 70, 79, 91, and 96 of the Useful Reference Series.

An index to handicraft materials

appearing in books and periodicals. Arranged by subject.

498 Reinfeld, Fred. Catalogue of the world's most popular coins. Expanded ed. rev. by Burton Hobson. Doubleday, 1971. 288p. $8.95.
Modern and ancient coins and their values. Arranged by country with historical notes about each. Many illustrations. Includes those coins most sought by collectors and most likely to increase in value.

499 Scott Publishing Co. Scott's Standard postage stamp catalogue. Scott, 1868– . Annual. 2v. in 1. $17.
Gives minute details—such as date of issue, design, denomination, color, perforation, and watermark—on all the stamps of the world. Most of the stamps are priced. Illustrated.

500 Taxay, Don. The comprehensive catalogue and encyclopedia of United States coins. Scott, 1971. 397p. $15.
Systematic listings of all coinages issued in this country from colonial days to the present with price quotations. Illustrated. No index but a detailed table of contents.

13 Language

General Works

501 Mencken, Henry Louis. American language: an inquiry into the development of English in the United States. 4th ed. and the two supplements, abridged, with annotations and new material by Raven I. McDavid, Jr. 1st abr. ed. Knopf, 1963. 777p. $12.95.

A historical account covering pronunciation, spelling, usage, American and English, and including words, phrases, proper names, slang, etc. Readable. Bibliographical footnotes. This is a distillation of the author's three-volume set, with some updating to show recent changes in the language.

Dictionaries

502 American Heritage dictionary of the English language, ed. by William Morris. American Heritage and Houghton Mifflin, 1969. 1550p. $7.95; thumb-indexed $8.95; deluxe $12.50.

Seeks to take up a middle ground between permissiveness and prescriptive authority. 155,000 entries and 800 usage notes. Traces etymologies back to proto-Indo-European.

503 Americanisms, a dictionary of selected Americanisms on historical principles, by Mitford M. Mathews. Univ. of Chicago Pr., 1966. 304p. $5.95; paper $1.95.

An abridgment of *A Dictionary of Americanisms on Historical Principles,* 1951. Contains words originating elsewhere but deriving new meanings in America. Bibliography.

504 Funk and Wagnalls Standard dictionary of the English language. International ed. Funk and Wagnalls (distr. by Crowell), 1969. 2v. $35; 1v. ed. $24.50.

Not exhaustive, but useful with Webster's Third because of its discriminative comment. Aims to keep up with new vocabulary, especially with scientific and technical terms, and includes proper names and foreign phrases all in one alphabet.

505 Murray, *Sir* James Augustus Henry, ed. Shorter Oxford English dictionary on historical principles. Prepared by William Little, H. W. Fowler, J. Coulson. Rev. and ed. by C. T. Onions. 3d ed. with addenda. Oxford Univ. Pr., 1962. 2515p. $30; 2v. ed. $35.

Although this is the abridged edition of the *Oxford English Dictionary,* it serves also as a supplement to it because of the addition of new words.

506 Random House dictionary of the English language. Jess Stein, ed.

in chief. Random House, 1966. 2059p. $30.

An attempt to catch up with our expanding vocabulary. Not exhaustive. Definitions are more informal than those in Webster's Unabridged. Lists important plays, books, and persons, and adds useful tables of volcanoes, ocean depths, rivers by length, etc. Includes an atlas and concise dictionaries of Spanish, French, German, and Italian.

507 Webster's New World dictionary of the American language. 2d college ed. David B. Guralnik, ed. in chief. World, 1970. 1692p. $8.95.

In one alphabet includes proper names, place names, foreign phrases, etc. Etymologies given first, followed by definitions in chronological order. Usage labels. Americanisms are denoted by a star.

508 Webster's Third new international dictionary of the English language, unabridged. Ed. in chief, Philip Babcock Gove and the Merriam-Webster editorial staff. Merriam, 1967. 2728p. $49.50; 2v. ed. $55.

Often criticized for its lack of preferred usage and for its acceptance of words not usually regarded as proper English. Libraries will wish to retain the second edition as well.

Abbreviations and Acronyms

509 De Sola, Ralph. Abbreviations dictionary: abbreviations, acronyms, contractions, signs & symbols defined, including civil and military time signals, Greek alphabet, international civil aircraft markings, numbered abbreviations, proofreader's marks, punctuation and diacritical marks, radio alphabet, Roman numerals, and ship's bell time signals, etc. New rev. and enl. international ed. Duell (distr. by Hawthorn), 1967. 298p. $9.95.

A useful but less comprehensive work than that published by Gale Research Company.

510 Gale Research Co. Acronyms and initialisms dictionary. Ed. by Robert C. Thomas and Ellen T. Crowley. Gale, 1970. 823p. $22.50.

Subtitle: "A guide to alphabetic designations, contractions, acronyms, initialisms, and similar condensed appellations; covering: aerospace, associations, biochemistry, business and trade, domestic and international affairs, education, electronics, genetics, government, labor, medicine, military, pharmacy, physiology, politics, religion, science, societies, sports, technical drawings and specifications, transportation, and other fields." Includes the most often encountered foreign terms, but is largely a compilation relating to the United States. The third edition adds 35,000 terms and such new areas as ecology, aerospace technology, and women's lib-
nyms and Initialisms (Gale, 1972. 129p.
eration. Supplemented by *New Acro-*
$15).

511 Pugh, Eric. A dictionary of acronyms and abbreviations. 2d ed. Clive Bingley, 1970. 389p.

A list of acronyms in management technology and information science. International in scope but British emphasis. Subject index.

Etymological and Special Dictionaries

512 Bliss, Alan Joseph. A dictionary of foreign words and phrases in

current English. Dutton, 1966. 389p. $6.95.

An excellent dictionary of those foreign words and phrases frequently used in modern English but which have not been anglicized in spelling or pronunciation. Fills a need which general dictionaries do not satisfy.

513 Holt, Alfred Hubbard. Phrase and word origins: a study of familiar expressions. Rev. ed. Dover, 1961. 254p. Paper $2.

Comments on the history and use of picturesque words and phrases.

514 Klein, Ernest. A comprehensive etymological dictionary of the English language, dealing with the origin of words and their sense development, thus illustrating the history of civilization and culture. Elsevier, 1966–67. 2v. $65.

The most inclusive etymological dictionary. Unlike other works in this genre, incorporates origins of given and mythological names.

515 Onions, Charles Talbut, and others, eds. Oxford dictionary of English etymology. Oxford Univ. Pr., 1966. 1024p. $16.50.

A modern and comprehensive etymological dictionary of the English language. Based on the *Oxford English Dictionary* and brought up to date. Lists some words of American origin, as well as personal and geographical names, and gives pronunciation.

516 Skeat, Walter William. Concise etymological dictionary of the English language. New and corr. impression: Oxford Univ. Pr., 1911. 663p. $4; paper $2.95 (Putnam, 1963)

Shorter than the author's *Etymological Dictionary* (below) and entirely rewritten. Gives derivations of words, but omits histories of their use. Appendix contains same information as in the larger and older work.

517 ———— Etymological dictionary of the English language. New rev. and enl. ed. Oxford Univ. Pr., 1910. 780p. $12.50.

Frequently reprinted. A standard work, scholarly and historical. For smaller libraries, the author's *Concise Etymological Dictionary* (above) may suffice. Appendix contains lists of prefixes, suffixes, homonyms, doublets, selected lists of Latin and Greek words, and the distribution of words according to the languages from which they are derived.

Rhyming Dictionaries

518 Johnson, Burges. New rhyming dictionary and poets' handbook. Rev. ed. Harper, 1957. 464p. $5.95; lib. bdg. $5.11.

Easy to use. Arranged by one-, two-, and three-syllable words. Defines and illustrates the various poetic forms and meters.

519 Reed, Langford. Writer's rhyming dictionary. Writer, 1961. 244p. $3.95.

Small but useful. Arranged by rhyme sounds of one-syllable rhymes, or words in which the final and accented syllable is a rhyme, and by two-syllable rhymes.

Slang

520 Berrey, Lester V., and Van den Bark, Melvin. American thesau-

rus of slang: a complete reference book of colloquial speech. 2d ed. Crowell, 1953. 1272p. $19.50. Comprehensive list, divided into sections for general slang and colloquialisms, the language of particular groups, and slang origins. Well indexed.

521 Major, Clarence. Dictionary of Afro-American slang. International Publ., 1970. 127p. $5.95.

A useful glossary, admittedly incomplete, of Afro-American terms including those that have diffused to white speakers as well as those that have remained the exclusive lexical property of the black language community.

522 Partridge, Eric. Dictionary of slang and unconventional English: colloquialisms and catch-phrases, solecisms and catachreses, nicknames, vulgarisms and such Americanisms as have been naturalized. 6th ed. rev. and enl. Macmillan, 1967. 2v. $18.50.

The standard work on the subject; historical approach.

523 ———— Dictionary of the underworld, British and American; being the vocabularies of crooks, criminals, racketeers, beggars and tramps, convicts, the commercial underworld, the drug traffic, the white slave traffic, spivs. Macmillan, 1961. 817p. $17.50.

Slang from America and the United Kingdom. "A dictionary planned on historical lines."

524 Wentworth, Harold, and Flexner, Stuart Berg, comps. and eds. Dictionary of American slang, with a supplement by Stuart Berg Flexner. Suppl. ed. Crowell, 1967. 718p. $7.95.

Quotations and definitions cover all shades of the meanings of words used by college students, beatniks, hoboes, and other social groups. Basic reference tool for American slang. New material contained in a 48-page supplement. Appendix contains word lists for affixes, reduplications, pig latin, onomatopoeia, nicknames, group names, and a selected bibliography.

Synonyms

525 The new Roget's Thesaurus of the English language in dictionary form. Ed. by Norman Lewis. Rev. and enl. ed. Putnam, 1964. 552p. $5.50.

An alphabetical arrangement of the Roget system of word classification, the purpose of which is to allow the user to avoid Roget's rather cumbersome multiple access approach. Useful for gathering a rich harvest of undiscriminated synonyms. It is not however a substitute for *Webster's New Dictionary of Synonyms* (no. 527) which remains indispensable for discriminating guidance through the difficulties of English synonymy.

526 Roget, Peter Mark. Roget's International thesaurus. 3d ed. Crowell, 1962. 1258p. $5.95; thumb-indexed $6.95.

The standard thesaurus or word book, arranged by ideas. This edition has the "pinpoint" index for locating the precise word quickly.

527 Webster's New Dictionary of synonyms: dictionary of discriminated synonyms, with antonyms and analogous and contrasted words. Merriam, 1968. 942p. $7.95.

Perhaps the most useful of the dictionaries of synonyms. Includes a Survey of the History of English Synonymy. See also no. 525.

Usage

528 Copperud, Roy H. Dictionary of usage and style: the reference guide for professional writers, reporters, editors, teachers and students. 1st ed. Hawthorn, 1964. 452p. $9.95; paper $3.50.
A helpful guide in avoiding errors of usage. Troublesome words and expressions are arranged in one alphabet along with major articles on collectives, punctuation marks, gerund construction, modifiers, possessive forms, etc.

529 Evans, Bergen, and Evans, Cornelia. Dictionary of contemporary American usage. Random House, 1957. 567p. $7.95.
A highly personal work displaying scholarship and wit. Considers British usage. The authors "are prejudiced in favor of literary forms," but list non-literary forms when there is evidence that they have been accepted. Arrangement of words, phrases, clichés, grammar, punctuation, etc., is in one alphabet.

530 Follett, Wilson. Modern American usage: a guide. Ed. and completed by Jacques Barzun and others. Hill & Wang, 1966. 436p. $7.50.
A helpful addition to books on good usage. Not so easy to use as Evans, and less compliant in the acceptance of new forms. Appendixes discuss confusion and conflict in use of "shall and will" and punctuation.

531 Fowler, Henry Watson. Dictionary of Modern English usage. 2d

ed. rev. by *Sir* Ernest Gowers. Oxford Univ. Pr., 1965. 725p. $6.75.
A modern revision of an older classic (1st ed., 1926). The text is still Fowler's but Gowers has pruned it of eccentricities and added new entries to discuss recent foibles and perversities of English usage.

532 The MLA style sheet. 2d ed. MLA Materials Center, 1970. 48p. Paper $1.25.
Contains style rules covering such matters as abbreviations, footnotes, and bibliographies. Widely adopted by scholarly and learned societies for the preparation of books and articles. The address of the Center is 62 Fifth Ave., New York 10011.

533 Turabian, Kate L. A manual for writers of term papers, theses, and dissertations. 3d ed. rev. Univ. of Chicago Pr., 1967. 164p. $3.50; paper $1.25.
A standard style manual for students. Adopted officially by many colleges and universities. Index.

534 U.S. Government Printing Office. Style manual. Govt. Print. Off., 1967. 505p. $3.
This is primarily a Government Printing Office printers' stylebook. The rules are based on principles of good usage and custom in the printing trades, but the work is valuable in answering all general questions. Includes a guide to the typography of foreign languages.

Foreign Language Dictionaries

Polyglot

535 Bergman, Peter M. Concise dictionary of 26 languages in simultaneous translations. Bergman,

1968. 406p. O.P. New American Library, 1968. Paper $1.25.

A list of 1,000 common English words under which are displayed equivalents in twenty six Romance, Germanic, Slavic languages plus several more tongues such as Japanese, Hebrew, and Swahili. Each language also has its own index referring to the serially numbered (1–1000) English words.

Chinese

536 Mathews, Robert Henry. Chinese-English dictionary. Rev. American ed. Harvard Univ. Pr., 1943. 1226p. $12.50.

Compiled for the China Inland Mission.

French

537 Larousse modern French-English dictionary, by Marguerite-Marie Dubois and others. Tudor, 1960. 2v. in 1, 768p., 751p. $7.95.

A good standard equivalency dictionary.

538 New Cassell's French dictionary, French-English; English-French. Comp. by Denis Girard. Compl. rev. Funk and Wagnalls (distr. by Crowell), 1970. 2v. in 1, 762p., 655p. $8.95; thumb-indexed $9.95.

Phonetic pronunciation. Includes proper names, tables of English and French irregular verbs, and English and French definitions. French Canadian terms have been added.

539 Nouveau petit Larousse, dictionnaire encyclopédique pour tous. Schoenhof, 1968. 1789p. $9.95.

Has color and black and white illustrations, portraits, and maps. Separate lists of personal and place-names. Title varies; the earlier edition (1959) was called Petit Larousse.

German

540 Betteridge, Harold T., ed. New Cassell's German dictionary; German-English, English-German. Compl. rev. ed. Funk and Wagnalls (distr. by Crowell), 1965. 2v. in 1, 629p., 619p. $8.95; thumb-indexed $9.95.

Useful appendixes of abbreviations, proper names, and irregular verbs.

541 New Wildhagen German dictionary, German-English, English-German. Follett, 1965. 2v. in 1, 1296p., 1061p. $19.95.

The English-German section uses phonetic pronunciation and has a list of geographical and proper names, and a section on German grammar. Scientific and technical terms are considered. The appendix in the German-English part features a pronouncing vocabulary of proper names.

Greek

542 Swanson, Donald C., and Djaferis, S. P. Vocabulary of modern spoken Greek; English-Greek, Greek-English. Univ. of Minnesota Pr., 1959. 408p. $5.

Includes useful sections on names of food and drink, weights and measures, and greetings for students or tourists.

Hebrew

543 Alcalay, Reuben. Complete English-Hebrew dictionary. Prayer Bk. Pr., 1962. 4292p. $18.95.

Considered the best dictionary of an evolving language. Gives idiomatic usage in both English and Hebrew and some proper names.

Italian

544 Hazon, Mario, ed. Garzanti comprehensive Italian-English; English-Italian dictionary. McGraw-Hill, 1963 (c1961). 2099p. $16.75.

The vocabulary of more than 100,000 entries furnishes pronunciation, idioms, and variations in usage. Abbreviations in common use in Italy and in English-speaking countries and proper names common in form in both languages are given in interesting appendixes.

Japanese

545 Kenkyusha's New Japanese-English dictionary. Ed. by Senkichiro Katsumata. New ed. Kenkyusha, 1954. 2136p. 2700 yen (about $18)

Japanese words are arranged alphabetically in transliterated form, followed by Japanese characters and their English equivalents. Supplemental tables.

546 Nelson, Andrew Nathaniel. Modern reader's Japanese-English character dictionary. Rev. ed. Tuttle, 1969. 1109p. $14.50.

Japanese characters precede the transliterations, which are arranged alphabetically. Extensive appendixes. More helpful than the Kenkyusha dictionary (above) for the non-Japanese interested in understanding the language as well as merely identifying words. Indicates traditional and modern forms.

Latin

547 Cassell's New Latin dictionary; Latin-English, English-Latin. Rev.

ed. Funk and Wagnalls (distr. by Crowell), 1968. 883p. $8.95; thumb-indexed $9.95.

Contains proper names in the general vocabulary with dates and identifying phrases. Sometimes brief biographies are included.

Polish

548 Bulas, K., Thomas, L. L., and Whitfield, F. J. Kosciusko Foundation dictionary: English-Polish, Polish-English. The Foundation, 1959–61. 2v. $25.

Phonetic pronunciation is used for English entries.

Portuguese

549 New Appleton dictionary of the English and Portuguese languages. Ed. by Antonio Houaiss and Catherine B. Avery. Appleton, 1967. 2v. in 1, 636p., 666p. $14.95.

Phonetic pronunciation is used. There are tables of abbreviations commonly used in Portuguese, foreign words used without change in Portuguese, numerals, and irregular verbs. Thumb-indexed.

Russian

550 Learner's English-Russian dictionary for English-speaking students. Comp. by S. Folomkiva and H. Weiser. 2d ed. MIT Pr., 1970. 655p. $12.50; paper $2.95.

Spanish

551 Crowell's Spanish-English and English-Spanish dictionary, by Gerd A. Gillhoff. Crowell, 1963. 1261p. $6.95; thumb-indexed $7.95.

Includes Latin Americanisms and many special vocabularies. Also has outlines of the grammar of both languages and an illustrated vocabulary builder.

552 Velázquez de la Cadena, Mariano, and others. Velázquez Spanish and English dictionary. New rev. ed. Follett, 1964, 1480p. $7.95; thumb-indexed $8.95.

A synopsis of Spanish grammar precedes the entries in this dictionary of equivalencies.

14 Literature

553 Siemon, Frederick. Science fiction story index, 1950–1968. American Library Assn., 1971. 274p. $3.95.

An index to 3,400 science fiction stories appearing in 237 anthologies. Author-title and title-author approaches as well as a bibliography of indexed anthologies.

554 Cook, Dorothy Elizabeth, and Monro, Isabel S. Short story index: an index to 60,000 stories in 4,320 collections. Wilson, 1953. 1553p. $16.

Supplement, 1950–54. Comp. by Dorothy E. Cook and Estelle A. Fidell. Wilson, 1956. 394p. $8. (Indexes 9575 stories in 549 collections.) Supplement, 1955–58. Comp. by Estelle A. Fidell and Esther V. Flory. Wilson, 1960. 341p. $8. (Indexes 6392 stories in 376 collections.) Supplement, 1959–63. Comp. by Estelle A. Fidell. Wilson, 1965. 487p. $12. (Indexes 9068 stories in 582 collections.) Supplement, 1964–68. Comp. by Estelle A. Fidell. Wilson, 1969. 599p. $16. (Indexes 11,301 stories in 793 collections.)

These indexes provide an invaluable clue to short stories in collections. Indexing is by author, title, and subject of the short story. A list of collections indexed provides a useful buying guide for the library.

555 Essay and general literature index, 1900–1933. Wilson, 1934. 1952p. $50. Subsequent v.: 1934–40, 1362p.; 1941–47, 1908p.; 1948–54, 2306p.; 1955–59, 1421p.; 1960–64, 1589p.; 1965–69, 1596p. $50 each. Annual subscription $20.

This index is published semiannually with bound annual and five-year cumulations. It indexes, by author and subject, essays appearing in collections from 1900 on. Thus it forms a useful adjunct to the card catalog of any library.

556 Granger, Edith. Granger's Index to poetry. Ed. by William F. Bernhardt. 5th ed. compl. rev. and enl. Columbia Univ. Pr., 1962. 2123p. $65.

———— ———— Supplement to the 5th ed., indexing anthologies from July 1, 1960 to December 31, 1965. Ed. by William F. Bernhardt and Kathryn W. Sewny. Columbia Univ. Pr., 1967. 416p. $35.

Symbols for anthologies indexed are given in combined title and first-line index. There are separate indexes by author and by subject.

557 Gribbin, Lenore S. Who's whodunnit. Univ. of North Carolina, 1969. 174p. No price available.

(University of North Carolina Library. Library Studies, no. 5)
A listing of all American and British authors from 1845 (the publication of Poe's *Tales*) to 1961 who have written book-length mystery and detective novels. Entries are under legal names with cross-references from pseudonyms and are keyed to bibliographic, biographic, and critical sources from which further information can be obtained.

558 Hackett, Alice Payne. 70 years of best sellers, 1895–1965. 3d ed. rev. Bowker, 1967. 280p. $7.90.
An entertaining and instructive bibliographic guide to American popular reading as reflected by best sellers. Title and author indexes.

559 Irwin, Leonard Bertram. A guide to historical fiction: for the use of schools and libraries and for the general reader. 10th ed. new and rev. McKinley, 1971. 255p. $10. (McKinley Bibliographies, v.1)
The first nine editions were compiled by Hannah Logassa under the title: *Historical Fiction*. An up-to-date revision of a standard classified list. Author and title indexes.

560 Johnson, Robert Owen, ed. An index to literature in the New Yorker, Vol. I-XV, 1925–1940. Scarecrow, 1969. 555p. $15.
———— ———— Vols. XVI-XXX, 1940–1955. Scarecrow, 1970. 477p. $25.
An index to imaginative literature or belles-lettres appearing in the *New Yorker*. In three parts: title listing; title listing of reviews of plays, books and motion pictures; a name index. Nonpersonal subjects are not indexed. The first series will be most useful for beginning with volume 16, the *New Yorker* has been indexed in the *Reader's Guide*.

561 Kuntz, Joseph M. Poetry explication: a checklist of interpretation since 1925 of British and American poems past and present. Rev. ed. Swallow, 1962. 332p. $7.50.
An index of those interpretations of particular poems which seek to identify the relationships of parts to each other and to the whole. The type of criticism here represented excludes considerations of antiquarian identification and literary influence. Arranged by poet and poems and gives citations to explicatory essays in books and periodicals. List of sources consulted.

562 MLA international bibliography of books and articles on modern language and literature. Modern Language Assn., 1921– . Annual. $15.
Now in four volumes a year: the first two being devoted to world literature by language, the third to linguistics and the fourth to pedagogy in foreign languages. A classified arrangement of material is used throughout. The definitive bibliography of a field which in its outer reaches impinges on an impressive range of related disciplines. Needed in all libraries which support original research or at least undergraduate collegiate curricula. Indexes.

563 The new Cambridge bibliography of English literature. Ed. by George Watson. Cambridge Univ. Pr., 1969– . v.2, 1660–1800, $37.50; v.3, 1800–1900, $37.50; v.4, 1900–1950, $49.50.
An up-dated revision of the older in-

dispensable classic, *Cambridge Bibliography of English Literature* (Cambridge, 1941–57. 5v. $85.) which should be retained, if owned, until the completion of the new series. Arrangement is first by form, e.g. poetry, novel, drama and then by chronology. For each author, cites collected editions, separate editions of individual works, and critical and biographical studies. Index in each volume. Volume 5 will contain a cumulative master index.

564 Sutton, Roberta (Briggs). Speech index. 4th ed. Scarecrow, 1966. 947p. $20.

The 4th edition incorporates all the materials in the three previous editions: 1935, 1935–55, and 1956–62, with additional titles in this field published from 1900 through 1965. Indexes speeches by orator, type of speech, and by subject, with a selected list of titles given in the appendix. Particularly useful for the amateur speaker in locating suggestions on how to prepare a speech and models he can adapt to his needs.

565 Walker, Warren S. Twentieth-century short story explication; interpretation, 1900–1966, of short fiction since 1800. 2d ed. Shoe String, 1967. 697p. $10.

————— ————— Supplement, 1967–69. Shoe String, 1970. 262p. $6.

An index to explications of short stories concerned with theme, symbol and structure appearing in books, monographs and periodicals. Arranged by authors and stories. Index.

566 Wilson, H. W., *firm, publishers.* Fiction catalog. 7th ed. Wilson, 1960. 650p. $9.

Differs from earlier editions in form. Part 1 is an author list of 4097 works

of fiction with full bibliographical information; annotations for each book are designed to show its nature. Part 2 is a title and subject index to part 1. Part 3 is a directory of publishers and distributors.

————— ————— 1961–65 volume. 1966. 299p. $11; price includes the four annual supplements noted below.

————— ————— Four annual supplements, 1966–69.

Primarily a selection aid, but also useful for readers' advisory service.

Encyclopedias and Histories

567 Benét, William Rose, ed. Reader's encyclopedia, 2d ed. Crowell, 1965. 1118p. $8.95; thumb-indexed $10.

A completely revised edition of a basic reference book useful in libraries of every size and type. Covers world literature. Entries on authors, titles, characters, allusions, literary movements, etc.

568 Encyclopedia of world literature in the 20th century. Wolfgang Bernard Fleischmann, gen. ed. Ungar, 1967–71. 3v. $98.

Consists of brief articles in dictionary format on all aspects of world literature. Cross-references. For American students its chief value is its coverage of European literature, treated in greater depth here than in other sources. A translation and adaptation of a German work *Lexikon der Weltliteratur im 20. Jahrhundert.*

569 Herzberg, Max J., and staff of Thomas Y. Crowell Co. Reader's encyclopedia of American literature. Crowell, 1962. 1280p. $15.

Essential facts about American and Canadian writers and writing from colonial times to 1962 are provided in this comprehensive one-volume reference book. Articles discuss authors, novels, plays, poems, stories, literary groups, newspapers, and places and terms associated with literature.

570 Literary history of the United States. Ed. by Robert E. Spiller and others. 3d ed. rev. Macmillan, 1963. 2v. in 1, 1511p. $17.50.

———— ———— Bibliography supplement. Ed. by R. M. Ludwig. 1964. 268p. $16.50.

The standard work on the subject, giving a comprehensive survey from colonial times to date and a selected bibliography. Supplemental volume provides bibliographic essays on various aspects of the field, including individual authors.

571 Oxford history of English literature. Ed. by Norman Davis and Bonamy Dobrée. Oxford Univ. Pr., 1945– . 12v. (In progress) v.2: pt. 1, Bennett, H. S. Chaucer and the fifteenth century. 1947. 326p. $8; pt. 2, Chambers, E. K. English literature at the close of the middle ages. 1947. 247p. $5.95. v.3, Lewis, C. S. English literature in the sixteenth century, excluding drama. 1954. 696p. $11.50. v.4, pt. 1, Wilson, Frank Percy. English drama, 1485–1585. 1969. 244p. $5.95. v.5, Bush, Douglas. English literature in the earlier seventeenth century, 1600–1660. 1946. 621p. $11.50. v.6, Sutherland, James. English literature of the late seventeenth century. 1969. 589p. $11. v.7, Dobrée, Bonamy. English literature in the early eighteenth century, 1700–1740. 1959. 701p. $11.50. v.9, Renwick, W. L. English literature, 1789–1815. 1963. 293p. $8. v.10, Jack, Ian. English literature, 1815–1832. 1963. 643p. $11. v.12, Stewart, J. I. M. Eight modern writers. 1963. 704p. $11.50.

Updates the *Cambridge History of English Literature* and, when finished, may supersede it. Excellent bibliographies. *The Cambridge History of English Literature* (Cambridge, 1907–1933, 15v. $95) should be retained if owned but, if not, its age and the availability of the new *Oxford,* now approaching completion, indicate that it should not be purchased.

572 Sampson, George. Concise Cambridge history of English literature. Rev. by R. C. Churchill. 3d ed. Cambridge Univ. Pr., 1970. 976p. $9.95; paper $4.95.

A survey based on the 14-volume *Cambridge History of English Literature.* This completely revised edition has new chapters on American literature and on the 20th-century literature of the English-speaking world. Sampson carries his discussion up to the '60s, covering such places as the West Indies and the new African states.

Dictionaries and Handbooks

573 Penguin companion to American literature. Ed. by Malcolm Bradbury, Eric Mottown, and Jean Franco. McGraw-Hill, 1971. 384p. $9.95.

Provides broad coverage of the most important writers in the United States. Emphasis is decidedly on the 20th century. Bibliographies. Cross-references. General bibliography. A second distinct section deals with the writers of Latin America and, in general, is limited to writers born after 1930.

574 Brewer, Ebenezer C. Dictionary of phrase and fable. 8th ed. rev. by John Freeman. Harper, 1964. 970p. $7.50.

One can use this for years and still be amazed at the amount of information it has on linguistic, literary, historical, biographical, and other subjects. The entry can be a phrase, name, title, quotation, proverb, or generic category (e.g., "Dying sayings"). In a class by itself, even if many of its entries can be found elsewhere with searching.

575 Burke, William J., and Howe, Will D. American authors and books, 1640 to the present day. Augmented and rev. by Irving R. Weiss. Crown, 1962. 834p. $8.50.

Concise and useful information about authors and their works, from the best to the least known. Includes related items such as literary societies, magazines, etc.

576 Nyren, Dorothy. A library of literary criticism: modern American literature. 3d ed. Ungar, 1964. 620p. $15.

Nyren, Temple (no. 586) and *Tucker* (no. 587) are comparable in that each either supplements or complements an older standard work, Charles Wells Moulton's *Library of literary criticism of English and American authors* (Moulton Publ. Co., 1901–5. 8v. Reprinted: Peter Smith, 1967. 8v. $10 each). *Moulton* is a compilation of quoted biographical and critical materials on Anglo-American authors from 680–1904. Arranged chronologically. Quotations are excerpted from biographies, critical studies, and book reviews. *Nyren* applies the *Moulton* formula to American authors writing after 1904. Index to critics. For an equivalent treatment of modern British authors, see *Temple* (no. 586).

577 Penguin companion to English literature. Ed. by David Daiches. McGraw-Hill, 1971. 576p. $10.95.

Primarily a biographical and critical dictionary of writers in the British Isles and of writers who used English in commonwealth countries. Entries are signed. Bibliographies and cross-references. General bibliography.

578 Freeman, William. Dictionary of fictional characters. Writer, 1963. 458p. $7.95.

Identifies about 20,000 characters created by some 500 authors over a six-century period.

579 Hart, James D. Oxford companion to American literature. 4th ed. Oxford, 1965. 991p. $12.50.

Includes short biographies of American authors, brief bibliographies, plot summaries of novels and plays, literary schools and movements, and brief entries for those social and economic movements that formed the background for much literary protest. Arranged by specific subject in dictionary format with numerous cross-references. Chronology index.

580 Harvey, *Sir* Paul. Oxford companion to English literature. 4th ed. Oxford Univ. Pr., 1967. 961p. $12.50.

English authors, literary works, and literary societies are stressed, but non-English persons and literary items are discussed when allied to English literature. The result is a handbook of widely miscellaneous, English-literature-oriented information.

581 Magill, Frank N., ed. Cyclopedia of literary characters. Harper, 1964. 1280p. $11.95; lib. bdg. $9.89 net.

Identifies and describes more than 16,000 characters, grouped under the title of the literary work in which they appear. An author index and a complete-name index facilitate ready-reference use. Also published under title: *Masterplots Cyclopedia of Literary Characters.*

582 Masterplots annual volume. 1954– . Ed. by Frank N. Magill. Salem Pr., 1955– . Annual. $8.50.

Extended signed essay-reviews of the 100 outstanding books of the previous year. Arranged alphabetically by title.

583 New century handbook of English literature. Rev. ed. Ed. by Clarence L. Barnhart. Appleton, 1956. 1167p. $14.95.

Based largely on the *New Century Cyclopedia of Names* (no. 705). There are entries for biography, allusions, titles, and characters. Somewhat more comprehensive than the *Oxford Companion to English Literature* (no. 580).

584 Opie, Iona (Archibald), and Opie, Peter, eds. Oxford dictionary of nursery rhymes. Oxford Univ. Pr., 1951. 467p. $10.50.

A scholarly collection of nursery rhymes with notes and explanations concerning history, literary associations, social uses, and possible portrayal of real people.

585 Shipley, Joseph, ed. Dictionary of world literary terms: forms, techniques, criticism. Rev. and enl.

The Writer, 1970. 466p. $12.95. Covers terms from all literary traditions which have evolved forms, techniques, and schools of criticism. Following the dictionary there are ten historical surveys of American and major European criticism. Bibliographies. No index.

586 Temple, Ruth Z., and Tucker, Martin. Library of literary criticism: modern British literature. Ungar, 1966. 3v. $45.

Designed to supplement Moulton's *Library of Literary Criticism of English and American Authors* (no. 576n) by providing excerpts from book reviews, biographies and critical studies pertaining to British authors writing after 1904. For an equivalent treatment of twentieth century American authors, see *Nyren* (no. 576).

587 Tucker, Martin, ed. The critical temper: a survey of modern criticism on English and American literature from the beginnings to the twentieth century. Ungar, 1969. 3v. $45. v.1, From Old English to Shakespeare, 582p.; v.2, From Milton to Romantic literature, 526p.; v.3, Victorian and American literature, 529p.

Designed to complement Moulton's *Library of Literary Criticism of English and American Authors* (no. 576n) by providing twentieth-century comment and criticism on the same Anglo-American authors, 640–1904, that are treated in *Moulton*. Contains a cross-reference index to authors and an index to critics. This work is in turn supplemented by *Nyren* (no. 576) and *Temple* (no. 586).

588 Wasserman, Paul, ed. Awards,

honors and prizes. 2d ed. Gale, 1972. 579p. $24.

An alphabetical listing of U.S. and Canadian awards recognizing achievements in all fields arranged by sponsoring organizations. Also includes international awards of interest to Americans. Exclusions are principally scholarships, fellowships, and study awards. Subject and award-title indexes.

589 Weber, Olga S. Literary and library prizes. 7th ed. Bowker, 1970. 413p. $10.95.

A classified directory of prizes, giving for each general background, requirements for eligibility, and a chronological list of recipients. Index.

Proverbs and Quotations

590 Adams, A. K. The home book of humorous quotations. Dodd, 1969. 436p. $10.

Contains approximately 9000 quotations distributed under a broad spectrum of subject headings and arranged alphabetically by author. Items have serial numbers to which the subject index and concordance refer. No author index.

591 Bartlett, John. Familiar quotations. 14th ed. Little, 1968. 1614p. $15.

A standard collection with quotations arranged chronologically by authors. Excellent index.

592 Bohle, Bruce, comp. Home book of American quotations. Dodd, 1967. 512p. $10.

Follows the model of Stevenson's *Home Book of Quotations* (no. 596) but is limited to quotations by Americans or about America. Index.

593 Evans, Bergen, ed. Dictionary of

quotations. Delacorte, 1968. 2039p. $15.

Usefully supplements the standard works, *Bartlett's* and *Stevenson*. Arranged topically, e.g. "chance," "charity," "cheating." Three indexes by topics, authors, and detailed subjects.

594 Simpson, James B. Contemporary quotations. Crowell, 1964. 500p. $6.95.

Supplements the standard collections of quotations. Contains more than 2400 quotable remarks made between the years 1950 and 1964. Categories include politics and government, business, law, science, the arts, travel, and family life. Separate indexes for source and subject.

595 Smith, William George, comp. Oxford dictionary of English proverbs. With an introduction by Joanna Wilson. 3d ed. rev. by F. P. Wilson. Oxford Univ. Pr., 1970. 930p. $16.

Provides an excellent supplement to the various books of quotations. Proverbs are arranged by the most significant word, with many cross-references.

596 Stevenson, Burton Egbert. Home book of quotations, classical and modern, selected and arranged. 10th ed. Dodd, 1967. 2816p. $35.

One of the most comprehensive and useful of the many books of quotations. Arrangement is by subject, with a very detailed index. A first purchase for any reference collection.

597 Macmillan book of proverbs. Macmillan, 1965 (c1948). 2957p. $25.

A subject arrangement of proverbs, maxims, and familiar phrases; a companion volume to Stevenson's *Home*

Book of Quotations. Has a very full index.

598 Tripp, Rhoda Thomas. The international thesaurus of quotations. Crowell, 1970. 1088p. $8.95; $10 thumb-indexed.

Uses an adaptation of Roget's classification of words for the purpose of exhibiting quotations under precise divisions of ideas. Indexes by authors and sources, by key words, and by categories.

Poetry

599 Preminger, Alexander, and others, eds. Princeton encyclopedia of poetry and poetics. Princeton Univ. Pr., 1965. 906p. $15.

Extensive articles, signed by modern authorities in the field of literary criticism, about all phases of poetry, i.e., history, types, movements, prosody, critical terminology, and literary schools. Bibliographies are appended to almost every entry.

600 Spender, Stephen, and Hall, Donald, eds. Concise encyclopedia of English and American poets and poetry. Hawthorn, 1963. 415p. $16.95.

Includes articles on techniques and form but is basically biographical. Many full-page portraits. Bibliography.

Shakespeare

601 Asimov, Isaac. Asimov's Guide to Shakespeare. Doubleday, 1970. 2v. $25.

Detailed explanations of the legendary, historical, and mythological backgrounds of each play. Volume 1 includes the Greek, Roman, and Italian plays; volume 2, the English plays. Indexes.

602 Bartlett, John. Complete concordance or verbal index to words, phrases and passages in the dramatic works of Shakespeare with a supplementary concordance to the poems. St. Martin's, 1965 (c1894). 1910p. $30.

An unrivaled work.

603 Campbell, Oscar James, and Quinn, Edward G., eds. Reader's encyclopedia of Shakespeare. Crowell, 1966. 1014p. $15.

A compendium of criticism and information on all aspects of Shakespeare's works. Sources are given at the end of many articles. Among the appendixes are a chronology of events related to the life and works of Shakespeare, transcripts of documents, genealogical table of Houses of York and Lancaster, and a 30-page selected bibliography.

604 Halliday, Frank Ernest. Shakespeare companion, 1564–1964. rev. ed. Schocken, 1964. 569p. $12; paper, 565p. $2.65 (Penguin).

Discusses persons, plays, characters, and theater contemporary to Shakespeare, as well as matters pertaining to Shakespeare himself. Also contains genealogical tables of the Shakespeare family, and of the families in Shakespeare's historical plays. Bibliography and illustrations are in the back.

605 Onions, Charles T. Shakespeare glossary. 2d rev. ed. Oxford Univ. Pr., 1963. 264p. $5.

Gives definitions and illustrations of words or senses of words now obsolete, explanations involving unfamiliar allusions, and proper names. A six-page addendum has been made to the 1919 edition.

606 Stevenson, Burton Egbert. Home book of Shakespeare quotations. Scribner's, 1965 (c1937). 2055p. $22.50 (by subscription only)

A subject guide with exact citations to the Globe edition of Shakespeare's plays and poems. A concordance is also provided.

National Literature

General

607 Lang, David Marshall, ed. Guide to Eastern literatures. Praeger, 1971. 501p. $15.

Intended to bring to the Western reader's attention salient facts on Eastern literatures and individual authors and to relate these to the cultural histories of the nations of which they are a part. The East is interpreted to encompass the Near and Middle East in addition to Asia. Signed contributions. Index.

608 Penguin companion to classical, Oriental and African literature. Ed. by D. M. Lang and D. R. Dudley. McGraw-Hill, 1969. 361p. $9.95.

Presents in dictionary format brief specific subject entries for authors, schools, movements, literary forms, philosophic doctrines. Entries are signed. Numerous cross-references. Bibliographies.

609 Penguin companion to European literature. Ed. by Anthony Thorlby. McGraw-Hill, 1969. 908p. $11.95.

A biographical and critical dictionary of the most important European writers. Bibliographies include translations of principal works. Signed contributions. Guide to entries by language and country.

French

610 Harvey, *Sir* Paul, and Heseltine, Janet E., eds. Oxford companion to French literature. Oxford Univ. Pr., 1959. 771p. $12.50.

6000 entries of varying length encompass the range of French literature up to World War II and discuss some history, philosophy, and science. Works are listed with dates of first publication. Cross references. Appended bibliography.

German

611 Rose, Ernst. History of German literature. New York Univ. Pr., 1960. 353p. $7.50; paper $2.75.

A literary history developed to show the effect of history on literature and vice versa. Selective bibliography of works of and about the literature in translation. Index.

Italian

612 Wilkins, Ernest Hatch. History of Italian literature. Harvard Univ. Pr., 1954. 523p. $10.

A brief survey, from the thirteenth century to the mid-twentieth, of Italian literature "of particular interest to the English-speaking world." Some biographical information together with critical interpretation of the work. Listing of authors *not* treated and of literary periods; bibliography of books in English about Italian literature. Indexed.

Russian

613 Mirsky, Dmitrii S. History of

Russian literature. Ed. by Francis J. Whitfield. Knopf, 1949, 1966. 515p. $7.95; paper $1.95 (Vintage); lib. bdg. $2.30.
Eleventh-century to early twentieth-century poetry, drama, and fiction. Biographical details and critical commentary are given. Extensively indexed.

614 Slonim, Marc. Soviet Russian literature: writers and problems. Oxford Univ. Pr., 1964. 365p. $8.95. Rev. ed. (1967) paper $2.25.
Major, widely known authors are discussed in chapters devoted entirely to them, while trends and cultural influences, together with critical comment on minor writers, are dealt with separately. Works are not indexed by title, but under author's name. Notes listed and a selected bibliography of available English translations and criticism.

Spanish

615 Chandler, Richard E., and Schwartz, Kessel. New history of Spanish literature. Louisiana State Univ. Pr., 1961. 696p. $10.
Cultural background, geography, and language formation are discussed as a setting for a complete history of types of Spanish literature—poetry, drama, fiction, and nonfiction prose. Appendixes include a general historical chronology. Bibliography and extensive index.

Spanish-American

616 Anderson-Imbert, Enrique. Spanish American literature: a history. Rev. by Elaine Malley. Trans. by John V. Falconieri. 2d. ed. rev. and

enl. Wayne State Univ. Pr., 1969. 2v. $11.50 each; paper $5.95 each.
Six centuries of literature written in Spanish in the Americas are considered in chronological order (v.1, 1492–1910; v.2, 1910–66). Historical and cultural framework discussed. Author index only. Selected bibliography.

Classical Literature

617 Feder, Lillian. Crowell's Handbook of classical literature. Crowell, 1964. 448p. $7.95.
Dictionary arrangement of terms, persons, gods, and places relative to the study of Greek and Roman literature. Famous books are analyzed individually and plays, scene by scene. Gives historical background. Extensive cross-references.

618 Harvey, *Sir* Paul. Oxford companion to classical literature. Oxford Univ. Pr., 1937. 2d ed. 468p. $5.75.
Useful for identifying geographical, historical, mythological, and political backgrounds that are relevant to the study and understanding of the literature of Greece and Rome. Extensively cross-referenced. Appendixes include maps, table of weights and measures, and a date chart.

619 Oxford classical dictionary. Ed. by N. G. L. Hammond and H. H. Scullard. Oxford Univ. Pr., 1970. 2d ed. 1176p. $26.
Brief, succinct entries in dictionary format on all facets of classical studies such as authors and themes. Signed contributions. Bibliographies. Index of names which are entries in the dictionary.

15 Geography, Travel, and Archaeology

General Works

620 Columbia Lippincott gazetteer of the world. Ed. by Leon E. Seltzer, with the cooperation of the American Geographical Society. Columbia Univ. Pr., 1962. 2148p. $75.

In a single alphabetic sequence, lists all the places of the world: political subdivisions and geographic entities. Variant names. Include such data elements as altitudes, industry, agriculture, history. 130,000 names and 30,000 cross-references.

621 The concise encyclopedia of archaeology. Ed. by Leonard Cottrell. 2d ed. Hawthorn, 1970. 430p. $16.95.

An encyclopedic dictionary of signed specific entries representing diverse phases of archaeology: sites and excavations, archaeologists, geologic epochs, research methods, new technical research tools, and many others. Bibliography. Classified list of topics.

622 Fairbridge, Rhodes Whitmore, ed. The encyclopedia of oceanography. Reinhold, 1966. 1021p. $25.

Covers all phases of oceanography, including closely related fields such as navigation. Signed articles. Bibliographies.

623 National Geographic magazine. Cumulative index, 1899 to 1969. National Geographic Soc., 1952–69. 3v. v.1, 1899–1946, $13; v.2, 1947–56, $13; v.3, 1957–69, $7.50.

Because of the wide appeal of the *National Geographic* and the excellence of its textual and illustrative material, its cumulative indexes are a great convenience, obviating protracted searches through the *Reader's Guide.* For years following 1969, consult the *Annual indexes,* the first of which covers 1970 (the Society, 1971, $1.).

624 Huxley, Anthony. Standard encyclopedia of the world's oceans and islands. Putnam, 1962. 382p. $10.95.

Lists the location and provides the dimensions of each body of water and island. Gives brief descriptions and history. Gazetteer and index.

625 Gresswell, R. Kay, and Huxley, Anthony, eds. Standard encyclopedia of the world's rivers and lakes. Putnam, 1966. 384p. $15.

Lists locations and for rivers their courses. Brief descriptions and histories of events associated with them. Gazetteer and index.

626 Webster's Geographical dictionary. Rev. ed. Merriam, 1969. 1293p. $8.50.
A good one-volume gazetteer, revised frequently. Gives pronunciation.

Atlases

627 Britannica atlas. Encyclopaedia Britannica, in cooperation with Rand McNally (distr. by Encyclopaedia Britannica Educ. Corp.), 1969. 556p. $35.
The 1969 edition is a new atlas, a project of ten years, presenting a completely new set of reference maps prepared by geographers and cartographers all over the world. The handsome, detailed, and easy to read maps are suitable for junior and senior high-school level and for adults. There are some 300 maps, with 65 map pages devoted to the United States and Canada, 47 to Europe, 50 to Asia, and 26 to Africa. Special sections are common scale maps of the world's major metropolitan areas and the "World Scene" showing population, natural features, mineral and energy resources, international trade, etc. Text is in four languages and glossaries are provided for translation of geographic terms. Keyed index. Continuously revised. Formerly called *Encyclopaedia World Atlas* (1942) and *Encyclopaedia Britannica International Atlas* (1965).

628 Medallion world atlas. Hammond, 1971. 672p. $24.95.
One of the most comprehensive of the Hammond atlases. Contains an alphabetical list of countries, states, colonial possessions, and other major geographical areas, noting for each its area, capital or chief town, and population, with the source and date of the latter.

The arrangement of the material in the bulk of the volume is by continent, then country, state, or province. All geographically related information pertaining to a country or region appears on pages adjacent to the ones containing a large multicolored political map (with its own gazetteer index) and a series of smaller typographical, economic, transportation, and other special maps. Statistical data for each include area, population, monetary unit, major language, and an illustration of its national flag in color. For the 50 states in the United States, information featured includes highest point, date settled, date of admission to the Union, popular name, name of state flower and state bird. A comprehensive 110,000 entry A–Z world index of all localities on the maps is provided, as is a glossary of geographical terms, information on map projection, and world statistical tables of oceans and seas, the principal lakes, islands, mountains, great ship canals, and the longest rivers. This revision contains the 1970 census figures, zip codes next to cities in the index, and four full-color sections. These are Biblical, world history, and American history maps, and a new unit called "Environment and Life."

629 National Geographic atlas of the world. Melville B. Grosvenor, ed. in chief. 3d. rev. ed. National Geographic Soc., 1970. 334p. $18.75.
A relatively new and excellent atlas designed to give maximum information of the kind one seeks in maps. Double-page-size maps permit selection of the most desirable map scale for each area. There are over 50 large political maps with some physical features, plus scenic and historical maps of the United States

showing National Parks and Civil War battlefields. Maps are clear, attractive, easily read, and descriptive text accompanies each geographical area. Special features are "Great Moments in Geography," "Global Statistics," "Population of Major Cities," and a temperature and rainfall chart for numerous cities around the world. Well indexed.

630 Rand McNally commercial atlas and marketing guide. Rand McNally, 1876– . Annual. $75 (by subscription).

Especially valuable for its excellent statistical and demographic data. Complete listings of county seats for each state and populated places. Provides commercial indicators of market potential for cities, counties, and regions. Reliable cartography. Index. The *Road Atlas* appears as a pocket supplement to the *Commercial Atlas*.

631 Rand McNally road atlas. Rand McNally, 1924– . Annual. $1.95.

Road maps of each state in the United States, Canada, and Mexico. Distances shown on the maps. Mileage charts.

632 Times atlas of the world: comprehensive edition. 2d rev. ed. Houghton, 1971. $65.

A superb achievement of the cartographer's art. Second edition includes up-to-date maps of the moon and artificial satellites. Thorough coverage of place names in the nationally approved forms. Excellent cartography and printing. Pages bound a little too close to the spine. Index.

633 U.S. Geological Survey. National atlas of the United States. Geological Survey, 1970. 417p. $100.

The first national atlas of the United States, this is a magnificent effort. In addition to demographic, economic, and socio-cultural maps which equal in cartographic skill those of any other atlas, it contains a unique section of "administrative" maps reflecting changing configurations of governmental districts, functions, and regions. Subject and place name indexes.

634 U.S.S.R. Glavnoe Uprovlenie. Geodeyii i Kartagrofii. World atlas. 2d ed. Moscenor (distr. by Rand McNally), 1967. 250p. $12.95.

An important atlas providing a preponderance of locational maps, i.e. those depicting communication routes, hydrography, relief, and population centers. The best atlas for maps of the Soviet Union. A Russian-sponsored translation.

Travel Guides

► While there is no series currently being published that can compare with the old *Baedekers*, there are many good ones available. Like the *Baedekers*, the *Michelin Green Guides* contain excellent maps of towns and cities which can be effectively used to answer reference queries on the location of buildings and sites and the positions of streets. It should be noted that the *Michelin* series is at present largely limited to Western Europe. For other countries and regions outside North America, *Fodor's Modern Guides* (McKay, 1953– , revised annually) offer a highly useful added resource. Ranging in price from $7 to $10, these annually revised volumes now cover countries, regions and cities in Asia, South America, North Africa, and the Middle East. For titles and prices consult McKay's catalog in *PTLA*. For North America, the titles listed below should suffice.

635 American Automobile Association. Tour guides: what to see and where to stay, where to dine—a catalog of complete travel information. The Association, 1971– . Annual. Available through membership.

Issued in twelve regional series for North America, e.g. South Central States, Great Lakes States. Uniform format for regional series. Arrangement by state and city. Include places of interest and places for lodging and dining. General travel information. Maps. Mileage charts, etc.

636 American Camping Association. National directory of accredited camps for boys and girls. The Association, 1933– . Annual. $2.

Title varies. Directories are arranged by state and alphabetically by name. Entries give all needed particulars for choosing a camp.

637 Farm and Ranch vacation guide. Farm and Ranch Vacations, 1971. 132p. $2.50.

A complete guide to vacations on farms and ranches in the United States and Canada. Arranged by state or province and then alphabetically by name. Full particulars given, including location, rates, and resources available.

638 American Hotel and Motel Association. Hotel and motel red book. The Association, 1886– . Annual $12.50.

The standard directory for hotels, motels and resorts, principally for the United States and Canada but with limited coverage for other countries.

Arranged geographically by state and city giving particulars on number of rooms, rates, address. No index.

639 Michelin et Cie. Michelin green guides. Services du tourisme Michelin (distr. in U.S. by French and European Publ., Inc.)

The green guides include places of interest, suggested itineraries, plans of tours and cities, etc. Background information on the country's political and cultural history, currency equivalents and conversion, brief lexicons of needed phrases. Approximately ten guides on Western European countries and parts of countries (e.g. chateaux of the Loire Valley) are available in either French or English editions. Eight additional guides are available in French-language editions only. Each is $3 or $3.50. For exact prices, countries and language editions, consult the distributor's catalog in *PTLA*.

640 ———— Michelin red guides. Services du tourisime Michelin (distr. in U.S. by French and European Publ., Inc.)

The red guides revised annually in March, provide current information on hotel and restaurant facilities which are graded according to a system of stars. Indications of average prices. Six countries in Western Europe plus Paris are covered thus far. Prices of guides vary from $3.50 to $4.50. For current prices and countries for which available, consult the distributor's catalog in *PTLA*.

641 Mobil travel guides. Simon & Schuster, 1970. 7v. $2.95 each. California and the West, Great Lakes area, Middle Atlantic States, Northeastern States, Northwest

and Great Plains, Southwestern States, Southwest and South Central Area.

Contains road maps, points of interest, restaurant and lodging accommodations, travel suggestions, etc.

642 U.S. Works Progress Administration. State guides.

These volumes were originally issued between 1937 and 1941. Although too few of them have been revised since that time, they continue to be exceedingly useful. Every library should have the guide for its own state, if it is possible to obtain it. Those libraries fortunate enough to have complete sets have an amazing body of well-ordered facts on tap.

643 Woodall's Trailering parks and camp grounds. Woodall Publ., 1967– . Anual. $5.95.

A directory of all park and camp grounds in the United States and Canada. Arranged by state and nearest city within states. Gives facilities and ratings. Maps and map index. Many special articles of interest to campers.

16 History

Chronologies

644 Everyman's dictionary of dates.
Rev. by Audrey Butler. 6th ed.
Dutton, 1971. 518p. $6.50.
Covers all periods of human history
up to the present day. In one alphabetic sequence, contains short entries
on particular subjects, narratives and
classified entries, e.g. soldiers, sieges.
Strong in the arts and literature. Index
to classified entries.

645 Carruth, Gorton, and associates,
eds. Encyclopedia of American
facts and dates. 5th ed. Crowell,
1970. 854p. $10.
Has a chronological arrangement, with
parallel columns to show what was hap-
pening concurrently in varied fields of
endeavor. Specific topics are found
through an extensive quick-reference
index.

646 Collison, Robert, comp. Dictionary of dates and anniversaries.
Transatlantic Arts, 1967. 428p.
$12.40.
Part 1 is in alphabetical order by name
of person, place, or event——very
brief information, serving merely to
identify and establish dates. Selective,
with British emphasis, but covering
events from earliest historic times
throughout the world. Part 2 refers to
the same events in calendar order.

647 Facts on file: a weekly world news
digest with cumulative index.
1940– . Weekly, with bound annual v. $200 a yr.
A weekly digest arranged under broad
headings, e.g. world affairs, national
affairs. Indexes published twice a month
and are cumulated throughout the year.
Three 5-year indexes also available:
1946–50; 1951–55; and 1956–60.

648 Kane, Joseph Nathan. Famous
first facts: a record of first happenings, discoveries, and inventions in the United States. 3d ed.
Wilson, 1964. 1165p. $18.
Compilation of first happenings, discoveries, and inventions in America.
Several indexes are provided: by years,
by days of the month, by personal
names, and by geographical location.

649 Mirkin, Stanford M. What hap-
pened when: a noted researcher's
almanac of yesterdays. Rev. ed.
Washburn, 1966. 442p. $7.95.
A calendar of dates with notable events
of each day listed in chronological
order by year. Emphasis is on events
of the nineteenth and twentieth centuries in the United States, but some
others are mentioned.

650 Williams, Neville. Chronology of
the expanding world, 1492–1762.
McKay, 1969. 700p. $12.50.

Political and international events are recorded on left-hand pages; on right-hand pages are recorded developments in the arts, sciences, scholarship, and sports for the same year. Detailed subject index. Supplemented by Williams' *Chronology of the Modern World* (no. 651).

651 Williams, Neville. Chronology of the modern world, 1763 to the present time. McKay, 1968. 923p. $12.50.
Political and international events are on left-hand pages; on right-hand pages are recorded developments in the arts, sciences, scholarship, and sports for the same year. Detailed subject index.

United States

Bibliographies

652 Handlin, Oscar, and others. Harvard guide to American history. Harvard Univ. Pr., 1954. 689p. $12.50; paper $4.95 (Atheneum, 1967)
Interpreting United States history in its broadest aspects, the references continue to be useful for students in spite of the book's publication date.

653 U.S. Library of Congress. General Reference and Bibliography Division. Guide to the study of the United States of America. Govt. Print. Off., 1960. 1193p. $7.
A valuable guide to every phase of American life. Excellent descriptive annotations. Brief biographies of many of the authors included.

Dictionaries, Encyclopedias, and Handbooks

654 Album of American history. Ed.

by James Truslow Adams. Rev. ed. Scribner, 1969. 6v. $120 (by subscription only)
A pictorial history of the United States from the first colonial settlements through 1968. Well selected photographs, drawings, prints, and pictorial reconstructions. Printed text consists of commentary on the illustrative matter and narrative connective tissue. Volume 6 contains a cumulative subject index.

655 Annals of America. Encyclopedia Britannica, Inc., 1968. 21v. $149.50.
Volumes 1–18 comprise approximately 2,200 selections from speeches, diaries, journals, books, articles illustrating and documenting the history of America from 1493 to 1968. Volume 19 is a proper name index to the *Annals* with references to volume and page. The last two volumes are the *Conspectus,* subtitled *Great Issues in American Life.* The *Conspectus* is a detailed analysis under 25 main headings, each with numerous subdivisions, of the cultural and intellectual themes with which both the *Annals* and American national experience itself have been pre-occupied.

656 Boatner, Mark Mayo. Civil War dictionary, a concise encyclopedia. McKay, 1959. 974p. $15.
More than 4000 brief entries, dealing with people, places, military engagements, and special subjects. Maps, diagrams, and an atlas of sectional maps covering the Civil War area are featured.

657 ——— Encyclopedia of the American Revolution. McKay, 1966. 1287p. $17.50.
Historical interests and activities dur-

ing the next decade will be increasingly centered on the American Revolution and its bicentenary. This dictionary, which also includes considerable material on events which led to the outbreak of war, should prove a useful first place to look when the questions start to come. Contains a bibliography and short-title index, and an index to maps.

658 Commager, Henry Steele, ed. Documents of American history. 8th ed. Appleton, 1968. 2v. in 1, 634p., 746p. $10.50.; paper 2v. ed. $4.95 each.

The best-known collection of basic documents "designed to illustrate the course of American history from the Age of Discovery (1492) to the present (1966)." Arranged chronologically, with 1898 as the dividing point.

659 Concise dictionary of American history. Advisory ed., Thomas C. Cochran; ed., Wayne Andrews. Scribner's, 1962. 1156p. $25.

This 1-volume abridgment of the 6-volume *Dictionary of American History* (below) is an excellent concise history, although not a substitute for the complete work. Bibliographies omitted, but there is an excellent index.

660 Dictionary of American history. James Truslow Adams, ed. in chief. Scribner's, 1958–61. 6v. and index v. $120 (by subscription only)

Individual entries in all of the volumes are signed, and most of them have a brief bibliography of more extensive works on the subject. Although the subjects appear in alphabetical order, the usefulness of the work is enhanced by numerous cross references and by a good index volume. The first supplement (1961, v.6), which covers the period 1940–60, was edited by J. G. E. Hopkins and Wayne Andrews.

661 Hurd, Charles, comp. A treasury of great American speeches: our country's life and history in the words of its great men. New and rev. ed. rev. and ed. by Andrew Bauer. Hawthorn, 1970. 411p. $12.50.

Arranged chronologically under broad rubrics such as "growing pains" (1833–65) and "depression, war and reconversion." Indexes.

662 Johnson, Thomas Herbert, ed. Oxford companion to American history. Oxford Univ. Pr., 1966. 906p. $12.50.

A very serviceable biographical and historical guide to American civilization. Biographical entries for major figures whether living or dead. Entries for literary movements, social protests, associations, and philanthropic institutions, etc. Exceedingly useful as a point of reference attack of the first resort.

663 Morris, Richard B., ed. Encyclopedia of American history. Updated and rev. Harper, 1970. 843p. $12.50; lib. bdg. $9.

Besides the general historical-chronological presentation, there are sections devoted to various special topics: the Constitution and the Supreme Court, thought and culture, American economy, science, and inventions, etc., also presented chronologically. Brief biographies of 400 eminent Americans are included. Maps and charts. Indexed.

664 Uniforms of the United States Army. Barnes, 1959. 2v. v.1, $17.95; v.2, $14.95.

Volume 1 by H. L. Nelson; volume 2 (Encore reprint) by Marvin Pakula. A reprint of the famous paintings of the U.S. Army uniforms from the earliest days to 1907.

665 U.S. National Park Service. National register of historic places. Dept. of the Interior, National Park Service, 1969. 352p. $5.25.

Arranged geographically by state and then county. The places are those which have received official designation as historic landmarks or which are preserved and maintained by the National Park Service. Entries provide information on the location and historical significance. Index.

666 Webster's Guide to American history. Merriam, 1971. 1482p. $14.95.

Part 1 of this three-part guide is a chronology of American history, 1492–1969. In parallel columns alongside each page are excerpts from various examples of Americana—fiction, poetry, lyrics, speeches and addresses, biography, and news articles. Part 2; maps and Tables of Statistical Data; part 3; biographical essays on more than 1,000 Americans. Comprehensive index.

Directories

667 American Association for State and Local History. Directory of historical societies and agencies in the United States and Canada, 1969–1970. The Association, 1969. 225p. Paper $10.

Libraries should acquire the latest edition of this biennial publication, which lists historical societies geographically, giving mailing address, number of members, museums, hours and size of library, publication program, etc. It is possible to locate societies devoted to a special phase of history through the index.

World History

Bibliographies

668 American Historical Association. Guide to historical literature. Ed. by George Frederick Howe and others. Macmillan, 1961. 962p. $16.50.

The best recent guide for general use, and source of many out-of-print titles now being reprinted. Especially valuable for its critical notes. Indexed.

Dictionaries, Encyclopedias, and Handbooks

669 American University. Foreign Area Studies Division. Area handbooks. Govt. Print. Off., 1961– . Irregular.

Funded by the military, the Foreign Area Studies Division has commissioned leading social scientists to prepare monographs on all those areas and regions of the world that are actually or potentially of interest to the U.S. Armed Forces. Most of the volumes in this series have been issued as U.S. Dept. of the Army Pamphlets in the "550– " sequence. They are available inexpensively from the Superintendent of Documents. Two examples of the Division's output are: *Area handbook for Vietnam* (1962. 513p.) and *Area handbook for Malaysia and Singapore* (1965. 745p.).

670 Dupuy, R. Ernest, and Dupuy, Trevor N. The encyclopedia of

military history from 3500 B.C. to the present. Harper & Row, 1970. 1406p. $20.

Organized in 21 chronological chapters surveying the history of war from the dawn of conflict through the Cold War, 1945–65. Attention is given to precipitating circumstances, the constitutions of armies and fleets, and to the technology of weaponry. Bibliography. Three indexes: general, battles and sieges, and wars.

671 Europa yearbook. Europa Publ. (distr. in the United States by Gale), 1959– . Annual. 2v. $60. v.1, International organizations and Europe. v.2, Africa, the Americas, Asia, Australia.

The best annual directory of the nations of the world. Covers for each such elements of information as demographic and economic statistics; constitution and government; press, trade and industry, publishers. Index.

Europa Publications also publishes three regional yearbooks: *Africa South of the Sahara* (1971– . Annual $28.50. Distr. by Gale) *The Middle East and North Africa* (1948– . Annual. $23.50. Distr. by Gale); and *The Far East and Australia* (1969– . Annual. $30. Distr. by International Publications Service). Analysis shows that these three regional yearbooks are compiled by reassembling elements from the *World of Learning* and the *Europa Yearbook* with only minimal elaboration of narrative material added to each. Unless a library has a strong special interest in any of the regions represented by Europa's three special yearbooks, purchase is not recommended.

672 Harbottle, Thomas. The dictionary of battles. Rev. and updated by George Bruce. Stern & Day, 1971. 320p. $12.50.

Originally published in 1905. Information given includes places, numbers of combatants involved, tactics used, and outcome. Bibliography. Index.

673 Hayes, Carlton J. H., and others. History of Western civilization. 2d ed. Macmillan, 1967. 940p. $9.95; 2v. ed. $7.95 each.

A good outline history, from the ancient Near East to the present day. Includes brief consideration of literary-artistic movements as well as political-military events. Illustrations. Adequate index. Appendix contains a select list of European sovereigns.

674 Langer, William Leonard, comp. and ed. Encyclopedia of world history: ancient, medieval and modern, chronologically arranged. 5th ed., rev. and enl. Houghton, 1972. 1504p. $17.50.

Events of world history concisely presented in an arrangement that is first chronological, then geographical, and then chronological again. Appendices list rulers, i.e., Roman emperors; Roman Catholic popes; British, French, and Italian ministries; and U.S. presidents. Geneological tables. The 1968 edition has added new maps and cross-references between sections, carried all events up to 1964, and completely rewritten the sections on prehistory, Greek history, and India in the British period.

675 Luttwak, Edward. A dictionary of modern war. Harper & Row, 1971. 224p. $7.95.

Concentrates primarily on the weaponry of modern warfare. Additional information on nomenclature and military organization. Brief entries in a single alphabetic sequence. Cross-references to broader, smaller and co-ordinate subjects.

676 U.S. Dept. of State. U.S. Dept. of State fact book of the countries of the world. Crown, 1970. 792p. Paper $5.95.

Contains succinct information on the world's countries under such headings as people, government, economy, and relations with the United States. Principal government officials and brief bibliographies. A reproduction and cumulation of the Dept. of State's series Background Notes. Supplementary information on international organizations.

677 Viorst, Milton, ed. Great documents of Western civilization. Chilton, 1965. 388p. $7.95.

The most comprehensive book of sources from the rise of Christianity to United Nations Charter available in one volume. Contains a reading list and an index.

678 Worldmark encyclopedia of the nations. Ed. and publ. Moshe Y. Sachs. 4th ed. Worldmark Pr. and Harper & Row, 1971. 5v. $69.95.

Factual and statistical information on 146 countries of the world exhibited in uniform format under such rubrics as topography, population, public finance, language, and ethnic composition, etc. Country articles appear in volumes 2–5 arranged geographically by continent. Volume 1 is devoted to the United Nations and its affiliated agencies. Illustrations, maps. No indexes.

Historical Atlases

679 American Heritage, *periodical.*

American Heritage pictorial atlas of United States history. McGraw-Hill, 1966. 424p. $16.50.

In the familiar *American Heritage* format, with many panoramas replacing simple maps, this atlas is more colorful and detailed than its predecessors.

680 Heyden, A. A. M. van der, and Scullard, H. H., eds. Atlas of the classical world. Nelson, 1960. 221p. $18.

An excellent atlas of the Graeco-Roman world, with clean, pleasantly colored, easy-to-read maps. Good illustrations. Available also is *The Shorter Atlas of the Classical World*, by the same editors (Dutton, paper $2.95).

681 Rand McNally and Co. Atlas of world history. Ed. by R. R. Palmer. Rand McNally, 1957. 216p. $8.95.

A standard historical atlas, arranged both chronologically and geographically by continent. Bibliography. Index.

682 Shepherd, William Robert. Historical atlas. 9th ed. Barnes & Noble, 1964. 353p. $17.50.

This edition contains all the maps of the 8th edition, revised and enlarged, and a special supplement of historical maps for the period 1929–55, prepared by C. S. Hammond and Co.

Africa

683 Daggs, Elisa, ed. All Africa: all its political entities of independent or other status. Hastings, 1970. 824p. $30.

A history and systematic survey of current status of Africa's fifty political entities. Arranged by status and by date of achieving independence. Illustrated. Index.

Asia and the Middle East

684 Adams, Michael, ed. The Middle East: a handbook. Praeger, 1971. 633p. $25.

Organized in six sections: general background, the countries of the Middle East, political affairs, economical affairs, social patterns, the arts and mass media. A broad-ranging historical and social science survey of the area. Differs from the *Europa* series in that this handbook is analytic and interpretive in contrast to the former's factual approach. Contributions are signed. Index.

685 Wilber, Donald Newton, ed. Nations of Asia. Hart, 1966. 605p. $15.

Signed articles on 24 Asian nations or areas, with pertinent facts stated briefly at conclusion of each chapter. Well illustrated, but most maps are small. Indexed.

686 Wint, Guy, ed. Asia: a handbook. Praeger, 1966. 856p. $25; paper $2.95 (Penguin, 1970)

Good coverage country by country, followed by essays on religion, art, literature, politics, minorities, world relations, and other aspects of modern world society. An appendix contains postwar treaties and agreements to 1960. Small black-and-white maps and a bibliography of American publications. Detailed index.

Australia and the Pacific

687 Pacific Island yearbook & who's who. Pacific Publ. (distr. by Tri-Ocean, 1932– . Irregular (latest ed., the 11th, 1972). $14.50.

For the various states and island groups of the Pacific, the yearbook covers commerce, trade, government, missions, languages, demography, ethnology, etc. Excellent directory source. Index.

688 White, Osmar. Guide to Australia. McGraw-Hill, 1968. 387p. $8.95.

Arranged by state, presents information of interest to tourists and travelers. For major population centers provides places of interest such as parks and gardens, galleries and libraries, churches, restaurants, etc. Illustrated. Index of place names.

British Commonwealth

689 Yearbook of the Commonwealth. H. M. Stationery Office, 1967– . Annual £5.5.

Now the publication of the Foreign and Commonwealth Relations Office. Thorough coverage of the constitutional history, present governmental structure, and current officers of all the countries that compose the British Commonwealth.

Canada

690 Canadian almanac and directory. Pitman, 1847– . Annual. $16.

The standard directory source for Canada including addresses and officers of associations, institutions, professional and trade organizations, government departments, etc. Statistical and factual data. Arranged alphabetically by topic. Detailed subject index.

691 Encyclopedia Canadiana. Grolier. 1970. 10v. $109.50 to schools and libraries.

Very thorough coverage of Canadian life in all its aspects—political, biographical, geographical, historical—

with good material on labor and industry, social sciences, and Canadian flora and fauna. Particularly recommended for those states bordering on Canada. Volume 10 contains an atlas with an index to the atlas. No general index to the set. The new edition features "a teaching guide to Canadiana."

692 Story, Norah. The Oxford companion to Canadian history and literature. Oxford, 1967. 935p. $15.

Designed "to provide a single source in which anyone reading a Canadian book in English or French can find an explanation of references that would otherwise be obscure"—Introduction. Articles vary in length from brief identifications to substantial essays. Numerous cross-references. Bibliographies.

Latin America

693 Martin, Michael Rheta, and Lovett, Gabriel H. Encyclopedia of Latin-American history. Rev. ed. by L. Robert Hughes. Bobbs, 1968. 623p. $15.

Dictionary arrangement of discrete subjects with numerous cross-references to related entry terms. Coverage ranges from pre-Columbian civilizations to the political ferment and international relations of the late 1960s. Though primarily political and historical, the work does include basic material on the religious, literary, and general cultural aspects of Latin America.

Other titles in the field are: Dana Gardner Munro's *Latin American Republics: A History* (Appleton, 1960, $7.75); John Francis Bannon's *History of the Americas* (2d ed. McGraw-Hill, 1963, 2v. $8.95 each); and Vera Brown Holmes' *A History of the Americas* (Ronald, 1950–64, 2v., $8.50 each).

694 Veliz, Claudio. Latin America and the Caribbean: a handbook. Praeger, 1968. 840p. $25.

Organized in five sections each of which deals separately with the countries of the area under the following section headings: general and historical; politics; economic affairs; social background; and fine arts. Contributions are signed.

695 South American handbook. Rand McNally, 1924– . Annual. $6.95.

A yearbook and guide to the countries and resources of South America, Central America, Mexico, Caribbean, and West Indies.

Russia and the U.S.S.R.

696 Utechin, Sergej. Everyman's concise encyclopaedia of Russia. Dutton, 1961. 623p. Paper $2.65.

An excellent, short-article encyclopedia of "contemporary Russia and its historical background," people, places, and things. Illustrations and portraits. Contains a "Systematic List of Entries" to related subjects.

17 Biography, Genealogy, and Names

Indexes

697 Biography index; a cumulative index to biographical material in books and magazines. Jan. 1946– . Wilson, 1947– . Quarterly (Nov., Feb., May, Aug.) with annual and permanent 3-yr. cumulations. $23 a yr.; v.1–7 (1946–67) available at $46 each.

Indexes biographical articles published after 1946 in approximately 1700 periodicals, current books of individual and collected biography, obituaries, letters, diaries, memoirs, and incidental biographical material in otherwise nonbiographical books. Index includes main or "name" alphabet and an index by professions and occupations.

General Biography

698 Current biography. Monthly except Aug.; cumulated annually. Wilson, 1940– . Annual subscription $12.

Biographical articles, with portraits and bibliographies, of newsworthy individuals of various nationalities. Continuously updated. Indexes cumulate; indexes for 1951–60 and 1961–69 are free. Annual volumes cumulate all the articles in one alphabet and add new information when necessary. These

Current Biography Yearbooks, not part of the annual subscription, are available, from 1946 to date, at $10 each. The volumes for 1940–45 are available at $24 each. Small libraries may find the monthly issues sufficient.

699 Dictionary of American biography. Scribner's, 1957–64. 11v. and Index. $260; Index (to v.1–10) $15 (by subscription only)

The standard reference for biography of important Americans who died before 1941. Each article documented with primary sources whenever possible. Each volume of this edition contains two of the original. Volume 11 consists of two supplements, bringing coverage up through 1940.

700 Concise dictionary of American biography. Ed. by Joseph G. E. Hopkins. Scribner's, 1964. 1273p. $25.

An excellent condensation of the *Dictionary of American Biography,* including only Americans who died before 1941.

701 Dictionary of Canadian biography. Ed. by Frances Halpenny. Univ. of Toronto Pr., 1966– . 2v. $15 each.

Each of these volumes contains about

600 entries discussing people who lived in Canada or are of Canadian interest and who died between 1000 and 1700 (v.1.) and between 1701 and 1740 (v.2.). The *Dictionary* also features a series of historical essays of importance to the United States as well as to Canada. Bibliography at end of each article, general bibliography, and index. The index to volume 2 is cross referenced to volume 1 and to future volumes. The entire set is expected to consist of 20 volumes, one published every two years. Les Presses de l'Université Laval, Quebec, publishes a French-language edition.

702 Dictionary of national biography, from the earliest times to 1900. Ed. by *Sir* Leslie Stephen and *Sir* Sidney Lee. Oxford Univ. Pr., 1885–1901, 1938. 22v. including supplement 1, $275. Supplement 2, 1901–11 (1912), $19.20; Supplement 3, 1912–21 (1927), $12; Supplement 4, 1922–30 (1937), $12; Supplement 5, 1931–40 (1949), $14; Supplement 6, 1941–50 (1959), $19.20.

Well-documented and signed biographies of notable inhabitants of the British Isles and Colonies who died before 1950. Bibliography for each biography. Every supplement has a cumulative index to all entries from 1901 on in one alphabetical sequence.

703 ———— Concise dictionary. Oxford Univ. Pr., 1953, 1961. 2v. v.1, From the beginnings to 1900, $12.50. v.2, 1901–50, $8.80.

A condensation and index of the parent set. Brief biographies of more than 30,-000 notable inhabitants of the British Isles who died before 1950.

704 Atlantic brief lives: a biographical companion to the arts. Ed. by Louis Kronenberger. Little, Brown, 1971. 898p. $15.

Includes more than 1,000 persons important in the arts in the Western world. Excludes only living persons. Lists subject's major works as well as critical and biographical studies.

705 New Century cyclopedia of names. Ed. by Clarence L. Barnhart. Appleton, 1954. 3v. $45.

Essential facts for more than 100,000 proper names of every description— persons, places, historical events, plays, operas, works of fiction, literary characters, mythological and legendary persons, etc. Volume 3 contains chronological table of world history, rulers and popes, genealogical charts, and prenames with pronunciation.

706 The New York Times obituary index, 1858–1968. New York Times, 1970. 1136p. $55.

A cumulation in one alphabetic sequence of the more than 353,000 names listed under "Deaths" in all issues of the *Times* from September 1858 through December 1968. A computer-based index developed to obviate the tedium of multiple volume searching for a single name. Indispensable for work in biographical reference. The *New York Times* obituary columns are the sine qua non of biographical information not only of prominent U.S. nationals but of the citizens of all countries of the world.

707 Prominent personalities in the U.S.S.R: a biographical directory containing 6,015 biographies. Comp. by the Institute for the Study of the USSR. Ed. by Ed-

ward L. Crowley. Scarecrow, 1968. 792p. $35.

An excellent "who's who" type of directory compiled by a very assiduous group of Kremlin watchers in Munich, Germany.

708 Radice, Betty. Who's who in the ancient world: a handbook to the survivors of the Greek and Roman classics. Stein & Day, 1971. 225p. $12.50.

A dictionary of historical, mythical, legendary, and literary names which are frequently alluded to in poetry, art, and music. Bibliography. Index.

709 U.S. Congress. Biographical directory of the American Congress, 1774–1961. Govt. Print. Off., 1961. 1863p. $17.74.

Lists executive officers, and gives biographies of members of Congress from the first through the eighty-sixth Congress.

710 Webster's Biographical dictionary. Merriam, 1970. 1730p. $9.50.

Useful for quick reference. Information given is necessarily brief, as more than 40,000 names are listed, from ancient times to the present. Pronunciation, dates, and chief contribution to civilization are given. Appended are a pronouncing list of "prenames" and some tables of presidents, sovereigns, members of the Hall of Fame, and the like.

711 Who's who. St. Martin's, 1849– . Annual. $32.50.

Emphasis is on Britons, but notables of other countries are included. Small libraries may purchase at intervals of several years without losing major value. Volumes as far back as 1962 are still available.

712 Who's who in America. Marquis, 1889– . Biennial. $49.50.

Abbreviated biographical information. This series, combined with *Who Was Who in America* and *Historical Volume* (no. 713), gives quick reference to facts about prominent persons in the United States from 1607 to the present.

713 Who was who in America. Marquis, 1942– . 5v. Historical volume, 1607–1896, 702p. v.1, 1897–1942, 1408p. v.2, 1943–50, 614p. v.3, 1951–60, 959p. v.4, 1961–68, 1236p. $34.50 each. v.5 in preparation.

These five volumes, plus the contemporary volume *Who's Who in America,* constitute the series *Who's Who in American History.* Chief use of the five historical volumes is for identification of people who were once prominent, whether or not their fame lived after them. Volume 4 indexes all five volumes. Additional editions will be brought out quadrenially.

Artists

714 Bénézit, Emmanuel. Dictionnaire critique et documentaire des peintres, sculpteurs, dessinateurs et graveurs, new ed. Brund (distr. in U.S. by Hacker Art Books), 1956–66 (c1948–55). 8v. $150.

A comprehensive work covering Eastern and Western art, including many minor artists from earliest times to 1947 for volume 1, and into the 1950s for volume 8. Arranged alphabetically. Reproduces symbols and signatures of the artists and lists chief works and where found.

715 Cummings, Paul. Dictionary of contemporary American artists. St. Martin's, 1966. 331p. $17.50.

Concise information about 697 American artists of the last 25 years who are represented in permanent collections. Includes also birth dates and pronunciation where deemed necessary. Illustrated. Contains bibliography.

716 Fielding, Mantle. Dictionary of American painters, sculptors and engravers. With an Addendum containing corrections and additional material on the original entries. James F. Carr, 1965. 592p. $28.50.

Reprint of the work published in 1926 with an addendum compiled by the publisher, including many new names. Brief biographies of nearly 10,000 artists.

717 Who's who in art: biographies of leading men and women in the world of art today. Art Trade Pr. (distr. in U.S. by International Publications Service), 1927– . Biennial. $15.

Contains names of prominent aritsts, critics, craftsmen, curators, etc. Also an excellent obituary section. Predominately British, although not exclusively so. A useful appendix lists monograms and signatures.

718 Who's who in American art. Bowker, 1947. Triennial. $25.

Sponsored by the American Federation of Arts. Previously part of the *American Art Annual*. Includes Canadian biographies, a geographical index, obituaries 1966–69, and a list of open exhibitions arranged geographically. The 1970 edition is in a new format.

Authors

719 Contemporary authors, the inter-

national bio-bibliographical guide to current authors and their works. Gale, 1962– . Annual. $25.

Brief and factual articles record all works published for a large number of authors hard to find in other sources. A new regular feature is the obituary citation. This includes lifetime dates, a line of identification, and a list of periodicals carrying the death notice. The 1971 obituary notes cover the years 1965 through 1970. Originally published quarterly (1962) and then semiannually (1963), with volumes double-numbered to indicate they were equivalent to two quarterly volumes. Beginning in 1971, published annually. Each volume is numbered as four units and is twice as large as the semiannual. Current volume is 25–28 (1971).

720 Contemporary poets of the English language. Ed. by Rosalie Murphy. St. James Pr., 1970. 1243p. $25.

A bio-bibliography of present-day poets containing information which is difficult to locate elsewhere. Arranged alphabetically by poet.

721 Kunitz, Stanley J., and Haycraft, Howard, eds. American authors, 1600–1900. Wilson, 1938. 846p. $10.

Biographies are written in an easy style. Brief bibliographies and portraits.

722 ———— ———— British authors before 1800. Wilson, 1952. 584p. $8.

723 ———— ———— British authors of the nineteenth century. Wilson, 1936. 677p. $10.

Companion volumes for biographical sketches of most British authors prior to 1900. Primary and secondary bibliographies and portraits.

724 ——— ——— Twentieth century authors. Wilson, 1942. 1577p. $18. 1st supplement, ed. by Stanley J. Kunitz and Vineta Colby, 1955. 1123p. $14.

Biographies of the best-known world authors of the twentieth century who have published in English. These short articles are accompanied by portraits and bibliographies.

725 ——— and Colby, Vineta, eds. European authors, 1000–1900. Wilson, 1967. 1016p. $20.

In the same format and style as the other books in Wilson's "Author Series"; covers 967 writers of 31 different continental European literatures, including Hebrew.

726 Magill, Frank N., ed. Cyclopedia of world authors. Harper, 1958. 1198p. $11.95; lib. bdg. $9.89.

Biographical details and critical and literary evaluations of 793 authors whose works are listed in Magill's *Masterpieces of World Literature*. Major works with dates. Bibliographic references are given at the end of each entry.

727 Untermeyer, Louis. Lives of the poets: the story of 1000 years of English and American poetry. Simon & Schuster, 1959. 757p. $7.95; paper $2.95.

From Chaucer to Dylan Thomas. Well indexed.

Librarians

728 Biographical directory of librarians in the United States and Canada. Ed. by Lee Ash. 5th ed. American Library Assn., 1970. 1250p. $45.

The successor to *Who's Who in Library Science*. Includes active members of the library profession, archivists, and information scientists.

Musicians

729 Baker, Theodore. Baker's Biographical dictionary of musicians. 5th ed. rev. by Nicholas Slonimsky. Schirmer, 1958. 1855p. with 1965 (143p.) supplement $25; supplement $5.

Very brief articles about composers, performers, critics, conductors, and teachers, arranged alphabetically under surname with pronunciation. Bibliographies.

730 Ewen, David. Composers since 1900: a biographical and critical guide. Wilson, 1969. 639p. $15.

Covers internationally 220 composers, either living or deceased, who have written music since the beginning of the twentieth century.

731 ——— Great composers, 1300–1900: a biographical and critical guide. Wilson, 1966. 429p. $10.

List of principal works and works about each composer accompany the biographies. Portraits. Appendixes contain chronological and geographical lists. Supersedes the author's *Composers of Yesterday* (1937).

732 ——— New book of modern composers. 3d ed. rev. and enl. Knopf, 1961. 491p. $10.

Similar in format to the author's *World of Great Composers from Palestrina to Debussy* (no. 734), this volume provides a cross section of the music of the past 50 years through presentation of 32 composers.

733 ——— Popular American composers from Revolutionary times to the present. Wilson, 1962. 217p. $8.
Brief, readable articles on about 130 composers. The title index of their compositions is worthy of mention. Contains a chronological list of popular American composers. Portraits.

734 ——— World of great composers from Palestrina to Debussy. Prentice-Hall, 1962. 576p. $15.
37 composers are discussed from four points of view: factual biography, the composer as seen by a contemporary, as seen by the modern music world, and as seen by himself. Includes bibliographical appendices and a detailed index.

735 Kutsch, K. J., and Riemens, Leo. A concise biographical dictionary of singers from the beginning of recorded sound to the present. Trans. from German, expanded, and annotated by Harry Earl Jones. Chilton, 1969. 950p. $14.95.
Lists many important 20th-century singers who are not to be found elsewhere. The basic requirement for inclusion is that the singer must have recorded his voice on phonograph records. Particularly strong for opera and classical music.

Physicians

736 Directory of medical specialists, holding certification by American specialty boards including listings, sketch additions and alphabetical index. Publ. by Marquis for the Advisory Board for Medical Specialists, 1939– . Biennial. $39.50.
Brief biographies of diplomates of 19 American specialty boards. Arranged first by specialty, e.g. dermatology, internal medicine, and then geographically by state and city. Biographies give only dates of birth, education, certification, experience, and present address. Index.

Politicians

737 Who's who in American politics. 3d ed., 1971–72. Comp. by the Jaques Cattell Pr. Bowker, 1971. 1171p. $37.50.
A biographical directory of political leaders in the Congress, the Executive branch of the federal government, state legislatures, state executive branches, mayors and councillors of major cities, and major party leaders without elective or appointive office.

Saints

738 Butler, Alban. Butler's Lives of the saints. Compl. ed. rev. and supplemented by Herbert Thurston and Donald Attwater. Kenedy, 1956. 4v. $39.50.
Incorporates most of the saints of the Roman Martyrology, including those recently canonized. Index. The following is recommended for substitution if local demand is slight: Donald Attwater, *Penguin Dictionary of Saints* (Penguin, 1965. 362p. paper $1.45).

Scientists

739 American men and women of science: physical and biological sciences. Ed. by Jaques Cattell. 12th ed. Bowker, 1971–73. 6v.

$35 each. v.1, A-C (1971); v.2, D-G (1972); v.3, H-K (1972); v.4, L-O (1972); v.5, P-Sr (1972); v.6, St-Z (1973).
Biographical sketches on 147,000 American and Canadian scientists active in approximately 600 fields of the physical and biological sciences. Title varies; through the 11th edition, 1965–68, this work was known as *American Men of Science*. For biographical information on scientific workers in the behavioral disciplines, consult *American Men of Science: Social and Behavioral Sciences* 11th ed. (Bowker, 1968. 2v. $66.) In both series, information stresses specific subfields of primary interest and publication.

740 Asimov, Isaac. Asimov's Biographical encyclopedia of science and technology. Rev. ed. Doubleday, 1972. 805p. $12.95.
From antiquity to the age of astronautics, includes the biographies of those scientists who have helped to shape our scientific and technological milieu. Name and subject indexes.

Sports Figures

741 Hickok, Ralph J. Who was who in American sports. Hawthorn, 1971. 256p. $9.95.
Arranged by sport, entries provide succinct biographical data on the most important luminaries of the American sporting world. Index.

Statesmen

742 Durant, John, and Durant, Alice. Pictorial history of American presidents. 5th rev. ed. Barnes, 1969. 370p. $12.50.
This revision, covering Presidents from

Washington to Nixon, is a photograph album with running text explaining the pictures. Gives additional information when events are dramatic, amusing, or far-reaching in historical effect.

743 Kane, Joseph Nathan. Facts about the presidents. 2d ed. rev. and enl. Wilson, 1968. 384p. $8.
From Washington to Johnson. In part 1 separate chapters for each president present data on a president's family history, elections, congressional sessions, cabinet appointees, vice president, and on highlights of his life and administration. Part 2 consists of charts and tables of comparative statistics on the president as an individual and on the office of the presidency. Portraits, facsimile autographs, and index.

744 Wise, Leonard F., and Egan, E. W. Kings, rulers and statesmen. Rev. ed. Sterling, 1968. 446p. $5.95.
Arranged by country alphabetically; entries provide complete listings of kings and rulers from the date of the country's foundation. Rulers listed are primarily of two principal types: heads of government and chiefs of state.

Theater Personalities

745 Biographical encyclopedia and who's who of the American theatre. Ed. by Walter Rigdon. Heinemann, 1966. 1101p. $82.50.
In spite of its price, this is a worthwhile purchase for a library of any size. Contents: New York productions (alphabetical by title) presented from 1900 through May 31, 1964; complete playbills since 1959 for New York City and leading experimental and repertory theater groups, existing and extinct, in-

premieres abroad of American plays since 1946; complete biographies of most important living persons connected with each aspect of the American theater; biographies of American theater groups, existing and extinct, including production records; histories of New York theater buildings; record of major awards; a biographical bibliography; discography of original-cast recordings; and necrology.

746 Who's who in show business: the international directory of the entertainment world. 1969–71 ed. Who's Who in show business, 1971. 541p. $25.

Arranged in separate sections by specialty category. Information on agents and ancillary theatrical services. Illustrated. Index.

747 Who's who in the theatre: a biographical record of the contemporary stage. Ed. by Freda Gaye. 14th ed. Pitman, 1967. 1720p. $25.

While the British stage is emphasized, the biographical section includes many Americans, from George Abbott to Blanche Yurka. This Jubilee edition contains encyclopedic information on the London stage and a little on the New York one. Contains index of London playbills, Shakespeare playbills, notable productions and long runs, obituaries, etc.

Genealogy and Names

Names

748 Bauer, Andrew, comp. Hawthorn dictionary of pseudonyms. Hawthorn, 1971. 312p. $12.95.

A useful list of pseudonyms and legal names in one alphabetical sequence. Includes assumed names of writers and artists thought to be of the greatest interest to the present-day student.

749 Kane, Joseph, and Alexander, Gerald L. Nicknames and sobriquets of U.S. cities and states. 2d ed. Scarecrow, 1970. 456p. $10.

Containing more than 10,000 entries, approximately twice the number of the 1965 edition, the work is divided into four index sections: geographical by city with nicknames, nicknames for cities, geographical by states, and nicknames for states.

750 Payton, Geoffrey, comp. Webster's Dictionary of proper names. Merriam, 1970. 752p. $9.95.

Contains approximately 12,000 proper names in dictionary order. Admittedly a personal choice by the editor, the work fuses in one source information traditionally found in a wide variety of reference books: place names, myths, celebrated heros, infamous villains, titles of novels, plays and movies, acronyms, Biblical personages, nicknames, fictional characters, etc.

751 Shankle, George Earlie. American nicknames: their origin and significance. 2d ed. Wilson, 1955. 524p. $8.50.

Embraces a wide range of subjects: the sobriquets and appellations of persons, places, objects, and events in American life, past and present. Bibliographical footnotes.

752 ———— State names, flags, seals and other symbols. Scholarly Reprints, 1971. 524p. $22. (Reprint of the 1941 Wilson ed.)

Arranged by state, includes the complete symbology for each: birds, flowers, songs, seals, mottoes, emblems, etc.

753 Smith, Elsdon Cales. American surnames. Chilton, 1969. 370p. $9.95.
An examination of the origin of those surnames most commonly found in America today. Bibliography. Index.

754 ———— Dictionary of American family names. Harper, 1956. 244p. $6.50.
Gives derivations of more than 6000 family names, with variant spellings. The most cosmopolitan of the surname dictionaries, but the ascribed meanings are not documented.

755 Stevenson, Noel C. Search and research, the researcher's handbook. Deseret, 1964. 364p. $3.50.
A guide to the location of vital records in the United States, Canada, and throughout the world. Useful handbook not only for the genealogist (to whom it is primarily addressed), but also for the historian, lawyer, and librarian. L. G. Pine's *American Origins,* which offers excellent guidance to genealogical records outside the United States, has been reissued by the Genealogical Book Co. (1967, $10).

756 Stewart, George R. American place names: a concise and selective dictionary for the continental United States of America. Oxford Univ. Pr., 1970. 550p. $12.50.
A judicious selection of place names chosen in accordance with three primary standards of admission: well-known names, repeated names, and unusual names which are themselves objects of curiosity or controversy. As the subtitle implies, Hawaiian names, mostly Polynesian, are omitted.

757 ———— Names on the land, a historical account of place-naming in the United States. 3d ed. Houghton 1967. 511p. Paper $2.45.
The index to this book on place-names leads to a wide variety of facts on the origin of the names of towns, cities, and geographical features in the United States. Illustrated. Includes bibliography.

758 Taggart, Jean E. Pet names. Scarecrow, 1962, 387p. $6.
Suggested names for dogs, cats, and horses in that order for space devoted to main categories. Also considers naming problems for birds, fish, and insects. Dog section (by far the largest) is arranged by breeding country of origin and lists names in variety of standard and exotic languages. Bibliography, Index.

759 U.S. Immigration and Naturalization Service. Foreign versions, variations and diminutives of English names, foreign equivalents of United States military and civilian titles. Rev. ed. Govt. Print. Off., 1970. 53p. Paper $1.
This Publication M-131 of the U.S. Immigration and Naturalization Service is a catalog of charts "designed to aid the person who needs to know the equivalent of commonly used English given names." Some names are given in as many as 16 languages.

760 Wells, Evelyn. What to name the baby. Doubleday, 1953. 326p. $3.95.
The original title of this work was *A Treasury of Names.* It was compiled by a scholar, and although she gives no sources, the book has always been especially helpful in giving variants and

foreign equivalents of first names. Since styles in naming new babies change rather quickly, many libraries will wish to supplement this book with *Book of Girls' Names* (now out of print) and *Book of Boys' Names* ($6.95), both by Linwood Sleigh and Charles Johnson, and both published in 1963 by Thomas Y. Crowell.

Genealogy and Heraldry

761 Boutell, Charles. Boutell's Heraldry. Rev. by J. P. Brooke-Little. Warne, 1970. 343p. $12.95.

Since the first edition of 1863, this book has gone through many revisions. It is now generally regarded as the standard work of reference on heraldry, although the viewpoint is primarily British.

762 Doane, Gilbert Harry. Searching for your ancestors. 3d rev. ed. Univ. of Minnesota Pr., 1960. 198p. $4.95.

A general discussion of how to pursue the study and practice of family history, and how to record the information when it is found. Its reference value is in its bibliography and in its information on United States census records and state vital statistics. Also of use is its list of sources for records of soldiers of the American Revolution.

763 Filby, P. William. American and British genealogy and heraldry. American Library Assn., 1970. 184p. $10.

Provides in classified order a selected list of books which American libraries should have to meet the needs of genealogists. Does not list family histories as such but rather the basic bibliographies, indexes, manuals, and auxiliary aids needed to pursue genealogical research. Index.

764 Gough, Henry, and Parker, James. A glossary of terms used in heraldry. new ed. Gale, 1966. 659p. $14.50.

Reprint of the 1894 edition. In addition to definitions, includes many illustrations of heraldic symbols and coats of arms. Index.

Flags and Decorations

765 Adam, Frank. Clans, septs, and regiments of the Scottish highlands. Rev. by *Sir* Thomas Innes of Learney. 8th ed. Johnston, 1970. 624p. $8.40.

A reliable guide to the problems raised by Scottish tartans. Also an "encyclopedia of clanship," discussing Celtic culture, the highland forces, and the history, structure, insignia, heraldry, and statistics of clans.

766 Dorling, Henry Taprell. Ribbons and medals, naval, military, air force and civil. Philip, 1963. 301p. $4.35.

This new edition, a second impression with enlarged supplement, was prepared in association with L. F. Guille and reprinted in 1970. The ribbons, given for most of the world, are illustrated in color. The medals are described, their origin and purpose are given, and in many cases the entry is accompanied by an illustration.

767 Kerrigan, Evans E. American badges and insignia. Viking, 1967. 286p. $16.95.

Military insignia of the United States, illustrated by diagrams with explanatory notes on qualifications, corps, and rank.

768 ———— American war medals and decorations. Viking, 1964. 149p. $6.50.

Contains information and illustrations of decorations of honor and service medals given to personnel of the U.S. armed services, together with wartime awards given to civilians. Chronological table of awards with authorization, bibliography, index, illustrations.

769 Pedersen, Christian F. The international flag book in color. Trans. by Frederick and Christine Crawley. Morrow, 1971. 237p. $5.95.

The use of full accurate color, very important in flag identification, makes this a model of its kind.

770 Smith, Whitney. Flag book of the United States. Morrow, 1970. 306p. $12.95.

Well illustrated, provides substantial and accurate historical information on the flags of the nation as well as those of the fifty states. Index.

Index

Numbers listed refer to entries and not to pages. An "n" after a number indicates that the work is mentioned in the annotation.

Bernhardt, W. F., ed. Granger's Index to poetry, 556

Bernier, B. A., and David, C. M., comps. Popular names of U.S. government reports, 43

Berrey, L. V., and Van den Bark, M. American thesaurus of slang, 520

Besançon, R. M., ed. Encyclopedia of physics, 283

Best's Insurance guide with key ratings, 147n

Best's Insurance reports, life-health, 148

Best's Key ratings guide: property-liability, 147

Better Homes and Gardens family medical guide, D. G. Cooley, ed., 334

Betteridge, H. T., ed. New Cassell's German dictionary, 540

Bibliography of philosophy, psychology and cognate subjects, B. Rand, 102n

Biographical directory of librarians in the United States and Canada, L. Ash, ed., 728

Biographical encyclopedia and who's who of the American theatre, W. Rigdon, ed., 745

Biography index, 697

Biological and agricultural index, 267

Biological data book, P. L. Altman and D. S. Dittmer, eds., 278

Birnbaum, M., and Cass, J. Comparative guide to American colleges for students, parents, and counselors, 234

Blakiston's New Gould medical dictionary, N. L. Hoerr and A. Osol, eds., 332

Bliss, A. J. Dictionary of foreign words and phrases in current English, 512

Blom, E., ed. Grove's Dictionary of music and musicians, 439

Blue book of occupational education, 262

Boatner, M. M. Civil War dictionary, 656; Encyclopedia of the American Revolution, 657

Boger H. B., and Boger, L. A. Dictionary of antiques and the decorative arts, 399

Boger, L. A. Complete guide to furniture styles, 398

Bohle, B., comp. Home book of American quotations, 592

Book of boys' names, L. Sleigh and C. Johnson, 760n

Book of costume, M. Davenport, 425

Book of festivals, D. G. Spicer, 225

Book of girls' names, L. Sleigh and C. Johnson, 760n

Book of health, R. L. Clark and R. W. Cumley, eds., 333

Book of old silver, English, American, foreign, S. B. Wyler, 395

Book of superstitions, R. L. Brown, 90

Book of the states, 199

Book of wild pets, C. B. Moore, 306

Book of world-famous music, J. J. Fuld, 446

Book review digest, 24, 25n

Book review index, 25

Booklist, 12, 19n

Books in print, 2, 5n

Botkin, B. A., ed. Treasury of American folklore, 89

Boutell, C. Boutell's Heraldry, 761

Bowker annual of library and book trade information, 28

Bradbury, M., Mottown, E., and Franco, J., eds. Penguin companion to American literature, 573

Brady, G. S. Materials handbook, 323

Brandon, S. G. F., ed. Dictionary of comparative religion, 58

Breed, P. F. and Charms, D. de. Songs in collections: an index, 430

Brenner, M., Grazda, E. E., and Minrath, W. R., eds. Handbook of applied mathematics, 295

Brewer, E. C. Dictionary of phrase and fable, 574

Briggs, M. S. Everyman's concise encyclopaedia of architecture, 386

Britannica atlas, 627

Britannica book of the year, 55

British authors before 1800, S. J. Kunitz and H. Haycraft, eds., 722

British authors of the nineteenth century, S. J. Kunitz and H. Haycraft, eds., 723

Broadcasting yearbook, 313

Brown, R. L., Book of superstitions, 90

INDEX